VIRGINIA'S LOST
APPALACHIAN TRAIL

VIRGINIA'S LOST APPALACHIAN TRAIL

MILLS KELLY

THE
History
PRESS

Published by The History Press
Charleston, SC
www.historypress.com

First published 2023

Manufactured in the United States

ISBN 9781467153393

Library of Congress Control Number: 2022947087

Notice: The information in this book is true and complete to the best of our knowledge. It is offered without guarantee on the part of the author or The History Press. The author and The History Press disclaim all liability in connection with the use of this book.

To everyone in Southwestern Virginia who keeps alive the memories of the original route of the Appalachian Trail.

CONTENTS

MAPS

PREFACE

We just went up into the woods some place, set there and talked about the trail. It was [Dad] and me and a couple of boys from town. There was a schoolteacher who came with us once. She had made up a song about it, and we sang the song together. The trail was all [Dad] cared about. When he worked on the trail, he would hang his hammock between two trees in the woods and would lay trail in the mountains. Sometimes for weeks.
—Dorothy "Dot" Shifflet, age 101, describing being on the Appalachian Trail in Floyd County with her father, Shirley Cole, in the early 1930s

This is a book about the Appalachian Trail, but it is not a book about *that* Appalachian Trail—the one you think you know. The one maybe you've hiked on. The one hikers call the "Green Tunnel." The one generating 1 million Instagram photos per year. The one that is so popular these days that hikers are literally loving it to death. It's not a book about that trail.

Instead, this is a book about a three-hundred-mile-long section of the Appalachian Trail that almost no one now remembers. A part that vanished from the thinking of the Appalachian Trail's leadership in 1952, even though they had spent the previous two decades extolling its beauty and its unique geological and cultural features. A part of the trail that crossed the Pinnacles of Dan, described by Earl Shaffer, the first hiker recognized as what we now call a "thru hiker," as one of the two most difficult and most beautiful bits of the entire trail. A part of the trail that crossed the New River, not on a highway bridge in Pearisburg the way it does today, but rather on a rickety little flat-bottomed riverboat named *Redbird* a few miles north of the mill town of Fries. That three-hundred-mile-long part of the trail was 15 percent of the whole thing when Myron Avery, the chairman of the Appalachian Trail Conference, declared the trail completed in 1937. And then it wasn't any percent—just like that.

Unless you're from Floyd, Mayberry, Check, Meadows of Dan, Vesta, Fancy Gap, Fries, Comer's Creek or Flat Ridge, Virginia, or unless you're old enough to have hiked or worked on the Southwestern Virginia section of the trail before 1952, you just don't remember this part of it. You won't find descriptions of this lost section in any of the hundreds of books about the trail, except a couple of short paragraphs in Earl Shaffer's *Walking with Spring* or Gene Espy's *The Trail of My Life*. George Outerbridge devoted three sentences to the whole section in his account of his section hike in the 1930s. And if you dig really far down into the volumes of *Appalachia*, you'll find a little five-page essay by Avery that has nothing but good things to say about this part of the trail. Altogether, these descriptions add up to about eight or nine pages worth of words, set against the millions of similar words that have been written about the rest of the Appalachian Trail.

Because you can't read about it in the old histories of the trail, there are only three ways to learn anything worth knowing about the original route the Appalachian Trail took between Roanoke and Damascus, Virginia. The first is to spend a fair amount of time poking around in the archives of the Appalachian Trail Conservancy (ATC), the Appalachian Trail Museum and the Virginia trail clubs. The second is to just go to Floyd, Patrick, Carroll, Grayson and Washington Counties and just start asking around. If you follow the route of the "Old Trail," as some folks still call it in those counties, and you stop in at stores, diners, post offices, gas stations and churches along the way and ask, people start to dredge up memories of the trail. Maybe not their own memories, but memories of a friend or neighbor whose farm the trail used to cross or whose uncle used to maintain the Old Trail or that guy named Charlie who comes in here sometimes. He talks about it. And eventually, you find yourself sitting with that friend or neighbor at the kitchen table, talking to them on the phone or writing good old-fashioned letters back and forth because e-mail doesn't work so well where they live. They tell you things about the Lost Appalachian Trail of Southwestern Virginia. Things you won't and can't find in any archive. Stories. Because Southwestern Virginia is a place where people organize and understand their lives through stories.

The final way you can learn about the Lost Appalachian Trail of Virginia is to go hike on it yourself, which is both easier and more difficult than you might suppose, especially if you're used to the Appalachian Trail as it is today. You won't find any white blazes on the trees, because the ATC and the trail clubs were mostly still using anodized tin signs in those days, and local trail maintainers pulled those down when the trail left in 1952. The few white blazes there were have long since faded away. When the ATC yanked the trail fifty-plus miles west to its current location on the far side of Blacksburg and ordered all those tin signs pulled down, at least one of the local folks who took care of the trail was so angry that he made a bonfire out in his backyard and threw in the trail markers from his section so they would melt away. Those markers didn't all get pulled down though. If you know where to look and what you're looking for, you can still find a few of the old tin markers nailed to very large trees, which weren't such large trees back in the 1930s when the signs first went up. Those signs don't have the familiar Appalachian Trail logo or the words "Maine to Georgia" on them anymore. These days, they are just rusted squares of tin, nailed up like brown diamonds on the trees.

If you do go to hike the old trail, the route you take will depend entirely on which year's *Guide to the Paths of the Blue Ridge* you choose, because the trail moved around a lot in those days. But if you find one of those old guides (they have a full set in the Floyd, Virginia Public Library), you can use it to walk the length of the Lost Trail without too much difficulty. The trail moved around a lot in this region because it was easy to move east of the New River. As it was located almost entirely on little-used gravel roads and abandoned roadbeds, all a relocation required was a change in the *Guide* to direct hikers down a different road and the moving of a few tin markers. New paths didn't have to be cut through the forest if the folks in charge locally decided that they didn't like a bit or a piece of the route they'd chosen. And those folks, and Myron Avery up in Washington, D.C., were always trying to find better ways to route the trail there to take advantage of the spectacular views along the Great Escarpment of Southwestern Virginia. Ultimately, the National Park Service had a lot to say about the trail's route east of the New River, as in 1933 the park service decided to slam the Blue Ridge Parkway right down along the same route that the Appalachian Trail was using, requiring a substantial relocation away from the road construction and, eventually, the cars. So, if you find a copy of the 1931 *Guide*, you'll take one route through Floyd, Patrick and Carroll Counties. But if the edition you find is the 1940 one, you'll take a very different route through those same three counties and will zig-zag back and forth across the parkway. Rather than relying on those books, though, the best way to hike on Virginia's Lost Appalachian Trail is to know someone so obsessed with the old routes that he just shows you where they all are. More about that guy later.

In addition to being a book about what was, this is a book about things that could have been. But it's also about how things that existed for decades never quite left and how people still remember those things because they remember a lot in the southern highlands of Virginia. They remember the stories of their great-great-great-grandparents who climbed up the Great Escarpment to take up land grants after the Revolutionary War, pushing aside the Cherokee who had lived there for centuries. They remember which of their relatives fought in the Civil War, and some try *not* to remember the ones who hid up on the mountain rather than going away to fight for the Confederacy. They remember when the chestnut trees all died, and they remember when the boys (and some of the girls) went off to war in Europe or the Pacific or Korea or Vietnam or Iraq or Afghanistan. They remember people begging for food at the back door during the Great Depression. They remember when their great aunt married that guy, the one no one liked much, and then moved down the mountain to Mount Airy or Winston for work. They remember the two old ladies who owned the antique store up the road, who always had a piece of candy for the children who came in. They remember the one-, two- or four-room school where they went until the big new schools were built. They remember the great flood of 1940. They remember Fourth of July picnics in the town park. They remember the Rhododendron Festival up on Fisher's Peak. They remember when they were teenagers and the local boys used to tease the girls at the only café in town.

And they remember hiking on the Appalachian Trail when it ran through their part of the state, or at least talking to hikers who passed through, as did Ralph Lee Barnard, eighty, speaking about hikers who stayed at his grandfather's farm:

> *Sure. I remember them. They would sometimes stay in the barn or just camp here in the yard out back. Some of them had the awfulest tales. There used to be panthers and such here and they always talked about the panthers. Or the bears. They talked a lot about the bears.*

People in Southwestern Virginia remember, even if the Appalachian Trail community doesn't.

This is a book about the Appalachian Trail as it was in its earliest days, from 1930 to 1952, and the traces it left across the landscape in one of the most beautiful and least visited parts of Virginia. And it's a book about what gets lost when people who live far away bring something important, something good, something exciting, to small communities that need and want connection to the wider world, and then those faraway people take the thing away. Just like that.

ACKNOWLEDGEMENTS

This book never would have happened without the support and assistance of many, many people. I first encountered the lost section of Virginia's Appalachian Trail in the archives of the Appalachian Trail Conservancy (ATC). The ATC's longtime publicist and archivist, Brian King, guided me through the various places in the archive where I might find information about the old trail and helped me understand Myron Avery's motivations and *modus operandi* when it came to getting the trail finished. Diana Christopulos, a past president of the Roanoke Appalachian Trail Club, helped me find many useful documents in that club's archives and read parts of the manuscript as it developed. Jim McNeely, who I discuss in chapter 5, devoted an entire day to driving me all over the old route of the trail and freely shared his incredibly detailed knowledge of the trail's many different routes through the region. A grant from the Virginia Foundation for the Humanities helped cover some of the costs of my trips to the area.

In Southwestern Virginia, I have been overwhelmed and humbled by the generosity and friendliness of everyone I have met there over the past three years as I researched this book. When I first began my research, Kathleen Ingoldsby, co-director of the Floyd Story Center, and Wayne Erickson invited me to stay with them whenever I was in town and have hosted me more times than I can count. Never once did they express frustration at my several trips there. Kathleen also helped me make a critical connection with Ralph Barnard and his lovely wife, Hope, who hosted me at their home not once but several times, telling me tales of the old trail and showing me pictures of the trail that they keep safe. Paula and Sally (Dixon) Rakes likewise have hosted me in their home several times and invited me to their family Fourth of July picnic so I could meet other relatives and friends who remembered the old trail. Doug Bell and his wife, Arlene, likewise hosted me at their home twice to discuss Doug's memories of the old trail, and Doug also took me on a hike to visit his grandfather's farm—where the trail ran right past the front door. Dylan Locke, owner of the Floyd Country Store, shared his insights about the musical history of the region. Richard Farmer, the mayor of Fries, Virginia, spent more than two hours telling me the history of his lovely town.

My friends Anne Reynolds of Wirtz, Virginia, and Jeff Ryan, the author of *Blazing Ahead*, a biography of Benton MacKaye and Myron Avery, read the penultimate draft of the manuscript. Any errors or omissions are my fault, not theirs. Our production team for *The Green Tunnel* podcast tested me with questions about the region, the old trail and the people I spoke with along the way. My close friends Charlotte Young and Calvin Cobb shared their home in Bethany Beach for a February that I used to write the final full draft of the book. The dean of the College of Humanities and Social Sciences awarded me a faculty development grant that defrayed some of the costs of my various trips to the region. Finally, my acquisitions editor at The History Press, Kate Jenkins, was unfailingly patient with me as I prepared to turn over the final product in a (somewhat) timely manner. My debts to everyone named here are too great to ever repay.

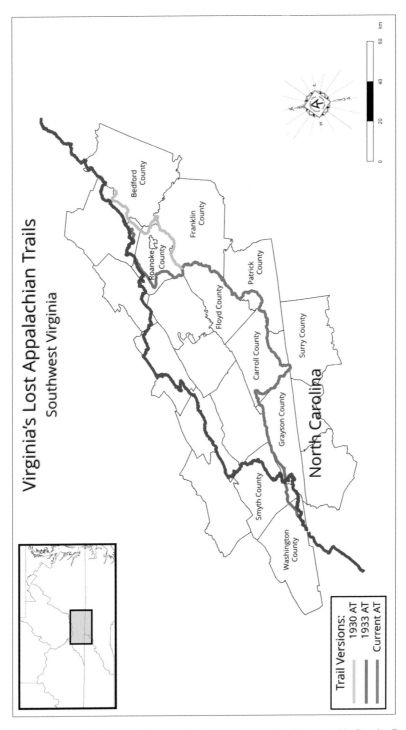

MAP 1 Routes of the Appalachian Trail in Southwestern Virginia. *Map created by Brandan Buck.*

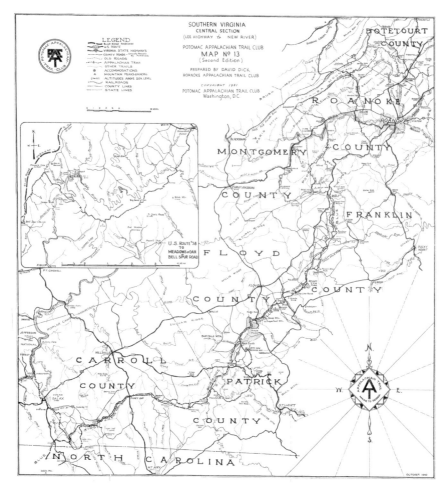

Map 2 Appalachian Trail in Southwestern Virginia, Eastern Half in 1940. *Potomac Appalachian Trail Archives.*

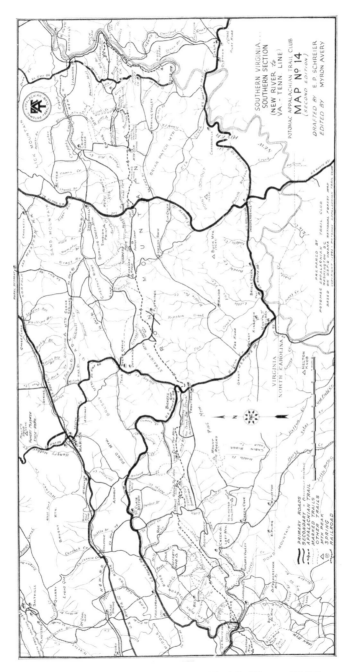

MAP 3 Appalachian Trail in Southwestern Virginia, Western Half in 1941. *Potomac Appalachian Trail Archives.*

BEGINNINGS

Sometimes, I think the state's just forgotten us here. I hope they haven't.
—Richard Farmer, mayor of Fries, Virginia, 2019

Not much happens in Fries, Virginia, these days. Not since 1989, when the mill closed, taking almost every single job in town with it. The people of Fries (pronounced "freeze") still haven't recovered thirty years later, which is not to say they aren't trying, just that they haven't yet. The high school closed the same year as the mill, and the population of what had once been a prosperous industrial town along the New River dwindled. The Norfolk and Western railroad spur that connected Fries to Pulaski and the rest of the world—the railroad that carried raw materials to the mill and finished products back north—was pulled up, and the old line was eventually turned into a branch of the New River Trail, a fifty-seven-mile-long state park running from Galax to Pulaski. That was the railroad that took mill hand Henry Whitter all the way to New York City in 1923, where he recorded "Wreck of the Old Southern 97" for Okeh Records, one of the first ever recordings of a country music song. And it was that railroad track that the town depended on.

Fewer than five hundred people live in Fries today, most of them working downriver in Independence, across the river and over the ridge in Galax or at the Volvo plant in Dublin, the one people in Fries still call White Trucks, even though Volvo has owned it for decades. There just isn't much work to speak of in Fries. So, they drive.

The New River at Fries, Virginia, in 1911. *Library of Congress.*

Standing in the park along the river today and looking back up at the town, you can see how it once was. Houses that would have been called neat and tidy lining streets that curve down to the river shore. A hotel. A bank. A few stores. Fries sits on a big sweeping bend of the New River, nestled between two ridgelines, and just upstream the dam still stands, the one that powered the mill. Turbines still turn in the old powerhouse, pushing electricity into the Appalachian Power grid, but those turbines are owned by a Swedish company now, and the mill was scraped off years ago, leaving behind a toxic waste site that took years to clean up. These days, there are some old tilted concrete slabs half out of the water below the dam and the usual tangle of tree trunks brought down by the spring floods. Once upon a time, though, Fries was a bustling town. All you have to do is look around to see that.

And people stay, despite the long drives for work, despite the feeling that they might have been forgotten by the bigwigs in Richmond, despite the fact that it's hard to see what the next big thing will be. They don't stay because they can't move. They don't move because, according to Richard Farmer, the town's mayor, "It's home. It's just home. It's what they know. What they feel good about. You walk down the street and you just know people. We live in such a beautiful place."

Almost no one in town remembers it these days, but from 1930 to 1952, the Appalachian Trail crossed the New River just north of town at Dixon's Ferry, right by the site of today's Route 606 bridge. There's still a small road named for the old ferry, parallel to the river shore, but there are no white blazes or diamond-shaped tin signs on the trees or fence posts or along the railroad tracks where they used to be. It's no wonder that almost no one remembers the trail. After all, it's been almost seventy years since the Appalachian Trail Conference (now Conservancy) decided to pull the Appalachian Trail out of this part of Southwestern Virginia and move it fifty miles north and west into the Jefferson National Forest. But for twenty-two years, it ran through the high mountain plateau of Southwestern Virginia and across the river just north of Fries.

Imagine for just a minute what it would mean for a town like Fries, where the only retail businesses are a Dollar General Store, a few little mom and pop stores, a nice little restaurant right on the river, a bright-red caboose where they sell soft serve and a post office. What if thousands upon thousands of backpackers hiked by, just two easy miles up the New River Trail each year? Think of all the money they would spend on ramen, Pop-Tarts, Knorr instant meals, protein bars, pizza, cheeseburgers and beer. Imagine a hotel, or a hiker hostel, maybe in the historic Washington Inn, that offered those smelly but cheerful hikers a place to stay, to do their laundry, to have a "zero day" that included a swim in the river or a kayak rental. Maybe there would even be a second café in town, sustained by thru hiker season, where diners could watch the way the river sparkles just as the last rays of sun are fading over the surrounding ridges. If they came on Thursdays, they could go to the free jam sessions at the Fries Theater and hear musicians from around the world come to play "old-time music" in the town where three of the earliest recording artists—Whitter, Ernest "Pop" Stoneman and Kelly Harrell—all worked in the mill but found time to take the train to New York to record their music.

Those hikers would have brought more than money to Fries. There would have been stories of places far away, accents from all around the world, and they would have shared what it was like to live in New York, Oregon, Berlin or Sydney. For towns like Fries that dot the Appalachian Trail today—places like Hot Springs, North Carolina; Damascus, Virginia; and Monson, Maine—all of these things happen, but that's because the trail runs through or close by their towns. Fries missed out on that, and then the mill closed, so nothing much happens there now. It's hard to be cheerful about it, but the mayor is and the town's slogan is "Pride in our

Past, Hope for the Future." Mayor Farmer grew up in Fries, went off to Vietnam after high school, learned about computers and had a career in IT. He and his wife retired back to the town where they grew up, where nobody locked their doors, where you didn't have to pay cash for things because you just signed your parents' names or used scrip from the mill at the store and where the sound of mill bell ordered everyone's lives until 1989. He worries about his town, but like any good mayor, he hasn't given up. Not at all. But it can be hard. "Sometimes, I think the state's just forgotten us. I hope they haven't," he told me in 2019.

Hikers often forget it today, or never even knew it, but when Benton MacKaye, a Harvard-educated forester and regional planner from Massachusetts, first proposed the Appalachian Trail in an essay in the *American Journal of the American Institute of Architects* in 1921, he wasn't just thinking a way to create a recreational resource. He also wanted the trail he proposed to help towns like Fries. As a regional planner, he'd spent a lot of time thinking about economic development, watershed management and the plight of poor rural and rapidly depopulating communities in the mountains of the East, and he came to the kind of crazy conclusion that a multi-state hiking trail would be a way to spur economic development and maybe even attract people back to these towns from the big industrial centers along the Atlantic Seaboard. Some of those people, he believed, would found cooperative farming communities that would lure other city dwellers back to the land.

MacKaye wasn't thinking that today's stereotypical Appalachian Trail hiker—young, scruffy, cheerful and mostly middle class, with an oddball trail name—would be who would spend time on the trail he proposed. Instead, his concern was mostly for the industrial workers of the great cities in the East. Those workers, MacKaye worried, were spending far too much time in dirty, sooty, loud, unruly and too often violent places, far from the peace and solitude of nature, far from the beautiful mountains that weren't really all that far away now that trains and buses and cars could take them into the hills. MacKaye's answer to what he called "the problem of living" was something so audacious, so crazy, that it caught people's attention. The Appalachian Trail would be, he said, a footpath in the wilderness, running more than 1,500 miles from the highest point in the South (Mount Mitchell in North Carolina) to the highest point in the Northeast (Mount Washington in New Hampshire), with subsidiary trails leading down into Georgia and up into Maine. Once completed, this trail would help people—industrial workers as well as the toilers in offices, in stores and, really, just about anyone who needed time in nature—reconnect to the land, to the forests, to the mountains, to fresh air and to peace. MacKaye wrote that the clean air of the mountain forests had "enormous health-giving powers," and if people just spent a week or two in those mountains, "there would be a chance to catch a breath, to study the dynamic forces of nature and the possibilities of shifting to them the burdens now carried on the backs of men."

Never could he have imagined the current popularity of his trail, with its 3 to 4 million annual visitors and the increasing thousands who attempt to hike it all in one year. I think that he would have been at least a little disappointed to find that most of those casual visitors and long-distance hikers were not taking some time off from factory labor, but were instead taking a break from their offices or their studies or were retired from white-collar jobs. Right from the start, MacKaye's Appalachian Trail was largely the domain of the middle classes who had the leisure time and the resources to take off into the hills for a day, a weekend or a week or two, who owned a car or had a friend with a car or could afford a train ticket and so could get to the mountains easily and when they felt like it. But he would have been pleased, I think, to see the positive impact that the Appalachian Trail has had on the small communities it passes through or near. And, I suspect, the fate of Fries, Virginia, would have made him truly sad.

As the Appalachian Trail enters its second century, it seems like a good time to resurrect the history of the three-hundred-mile segment of the

The Pinnacles of Dan in 1932. *Appalachian Trail Conservancy Archives.*

Appalachian Trail in Southwestern Virginia, at least for a little while, so we can remember the trail as it was, in its original form. When the ATC declared the trail completed in 1937, this section constituted more trail than the sections in Connecticut, Massachusetts and Vermont combined. And it included some of the most rugged, most isolated and most beautiful sections of the Appalachian Trail in its earliest incarnation. It passed through the towns and valleys where country music began and crossed some of the most unique geological features of the entire Appalachian Mountain chain. Because of all the road walking east of the New River that this section required, it wasn't to everyone's taste, but others came away entranced.

When the ATC's trail scout Roy Ozmer began trying to puzzle out the route in Southwestern Virginia in 1930, he was immediately struck by the beauty of the Pinnacles of Dan. "I know of no single spot in the Southwestern Appalachians, and this includes the Great Smokies, that is more wonderful and charming. It exceeds even the stupendous Nantahala Gorge," he wrote at the time. Two decades later, Earl Shaffer wrote that the Pinnacles were "the most rugged, and most spectacular segment of the Trail." W.H.T. Squires, a travel writer from Virginia's Piedmont who visited the area in 1928, gushed:

> *Here one stands on the edge of a gigantic gorge. Miles above the Dan comes leaping down in a long series of cascades. The river's silver thread is in large part obscured by the interlaced foliage of oaks and elms, poplars and hickories. The gorge is so vast, the depth so stupendous, the river so small that it would seem impossible for the Dan to have washed so vast a canyon. Perhaps the granite front of the Blue Ridge cracked at creation.*

Farther south and west, the trail's original route wound its way along the summits of the Iron Mountains, the highest in Virginia with the exception of the Grayson Highlands (where the trail runs today), most of which were well above 3,500 feet and some as high as 5,700 feet. Heading north, the Appalachian Trail does not crest the 5,000-foot elevation line again until it gets to New Hampshire. Unlike other sections of the trail that ran close to towns where hikers could find services like stores or post offices, much of the Appalachian Trail in Southwestern Virginia was truly isolated, even though almost half of it was on old roadbeds. Early hikers in this region often had to negotiate with local farmers to purchase provisions and were also pleased to find that some of those local folks, surprised by the novelty of someone hiking a long distance with a backpack on, would invite them in for meals, give them a room for the night or offer up their barn as sleeping quarters. Despite the stated aim of the ATC to build a chain of shelters from one end of the trail to another, only one trail shelter was ever built in Southwestern Virginia—an open stone structure perched on the edge of Rocky Knob, just a little south of the town of Floyd, built by the Civilian Conservation Corps during the construction of the Blue Ridge Parkway in 1937. It stands there still, a short walk uphill from the Saddle turnout on the Blue Ridge Parkway, mute testimony to the grand ambitions of those who planned to make the Appalachian Trail a permanent fixture in that part of Virginia.

The first blow that fell on the Appalachian Trail in Southwestern Virginia came in the form of the Blue Ridge Parkway. As in the newly formed Shenandoah National Park, the National Park Service decided to create a motorway in the mountains that would take newly car-owning tourists from north to south and back again along the spine of the Blue Ridge Mountains. It's not surprising that the planners in Washington decided to obliterate the already existing Appalachian Trail to build that road, as the scouts who laid out the Appalachian Trail in Virginia and North Carolina had already chosen the most perfect route for their trail—along the best ridgelines with the best views—and so what better location could there be for a road than along the Appalachian Trail's route? Despite their best efforts, the leaders of the ATC were no match for the power of the National Park Service when it came to working with the states to gain control of land and then build roads on that land. The park service had both money to buy the land and the power of condemnation if landowners chose not to sell, and so it didn't take the government planners long to gain control of the best strips of real estate along the edge of the Great Escarpment, pushing the trail off to the side. ATC chairman Myron Avery didn't love having the park service push his trail around, but he was willing to accommodate the parkway in the interest of getting the Appalachian Trail built and protected. If making peace with parkways was the price he had to pay, it was a price he was *willing* to pay. Benton MacKaye was in no way willing to pay that price, and it was this issue that permanently ruined his relationship with Myron Avery. In an angry exchange of letters between the two men over the issue of Skyline Drive, things were said that couldn't be unsaid and the two never spoke again.

The other blow to the trail in Southwestern Virginia was more self-inflicted. When the Appalachian Trail first began to appear on maps in 1925, the newly formed Appalachian Trail Conference decided to organize the work around local trail maintaining clubs. North of the Susquehanna River in Pennsylvania, many such clubs already existed, and all that was required was to encourage them to sign on to the Appalachian Trail project and work out agreements among them about who would be responsible for which stretch of the new trail and how that trail might take best advantage of existing trail networks. A few new clubs needed to be created in the Northeast to fill in the gaps between those preexisting clubs, with the single largest problem being how to extend the trail into Maine, but by and large, the raw material for a network of trail maintaining clubs was already in place. South of the Susquehanna, matters were entirely different. There were only a few similar clubs in the South, and they were mostly recent arrivals to the world of organized hiking in America. Thus, one of the earliest and most important tasks of the ATC was to encourage the creation of a slew of new hiking clubs in the South—clubs that could be responsible for scouting, blazing, building and then maintaining the Appalachian Trail as it wound its way down into Georgia.

Avery, the main driver of these efforts and soon to be chairman of the ATC, played an important role in the spawning of clubs across the South. He was the first president of the newly formed and Washington-based Potomac Appalachian Trail Club (PATC) and used the PATC structure to help organize clubs south of PATC territory in Lynchburg and Roanoke. Even farther south, he provided great encouragement to the founders of the Georgia Appalachian Trail Club, the Carolina Mountain Club, the Tennessee Eastman Hiking and Canoeing Club and the Smoky Mountains Hiking Club. Between them, these seven clubs were responsible for the creation and then maintenance of the Appalachian Trail south from the Susquehanna River to Roanoke, Virginia, and from Mount Oglethorpe in Georgia north to the Tennessee/Virginia border. That emerging network of trail clubs had just one big gap in it: from Damascus, Virginia, on the Tennessee line up to Salem, just south of Roanoke. Figuring out how to fill that gap in the trail between Damascus and Salem became a pressing problem for Avery in 1929.

When it came to Southwestern Virginia, Avery uncharacteristically found himself out of his depth. A government lawyer from Maine living in Washington, D.C., he knew no one in Southwestern Virginia whom he could call on for help. There weren't any hiking clubs in the region to which he could turn for assistance. There weren't even any substantial cities he could visit to look for collaborators. The furniture manufacturing town of Galax close to the New River was the only really substantial town in the region, and Avery knew no one there, which helps to explain why, in a 1929 letter, he referred to Southwestern Virginia as "our terra incognita." Damascus, at the far southern end of the proposed route of the trail, was a bustling lumber town, but in 1930 it had only 1,600 residents. Otherwise, the town of Floyd had fewer than 500 residents, as did Hillsville, the county seat of Carroll County. This region really was a place little known and far away to men like Avery. No one raised in Southwestern Virginia would be surprised to hear that a government lawyer from Maine living in Washington, D.C., would know nothing about their part of Virginia. Being invisible to officials in Washington was a way of life for those living and working in Appalachia, and Southwestern Virginia was even more invisible than other parts of the region because this part of the state had little or no coal and so the violence and disorder of the coal mining regions had largely passed the area by, keeping it out of the headlines and thus beneath the notice of Washington officialdom or the eastern media.

And then, one day in 1930, a letter from man named Shirley Leon Cole appeared in Avery's mailbox. Cole, the agricultural extension agent in Floyd, Virginia (about forty miles south of Roanoke), wrote that he and two friends had scouted a route for the Appalachian Trail from Roanoke to the North Carolina border and that they were in the process of forming a Southern Virginia Appalachian Trail Association that could take up the work of scouting, blazing, building and maintaining the trail in their part of the state. Avery's reaction was decidedly mixed, as will become clear in the next chapter, but Cole's proposal at least offered Avery a way forward in Southwestern Virginia. Over the course of the next three years, a mix of volunteers from the region—Floyd, Patrick, Carroll, Grayson and Washington Counties and the city of Galax—working at times with volunteers from Avery's PATC and at other times with volunteers from the Roanoke or Natural Bridge (Lynchburg) Appalachian Trail Clubs, along with help from staff of the U.S. Forest Service, managed to complete the trail from Salem to Damascus. This new section of the trail was one of the last unbuilt sections of the trail (Maine being the other), and with its completion, the Appalachian Trail was a big step closer to being done.

That three-hundred-mile section of the Appalachian Trail survived for only twenty-two years, just long enough to be inscribed in the memories of the people in the region, but not long enough to be similarly inscribed in the memories of those who ran the Appalachian Trail. As soon as they decided to yank the Appalachian Trail west and north into the Jefferson National Forest, this part of Southwestern Virginia essentially vanished from the narrative of the Appalachian Trail. You can't find it in histories of the trail. You can't find it marked on maps made after the 1950s. You can't find it in memoirs of the trail's key figures or in the Appalachian Trail Museum in Pennsylvania. But you can find traces of the Old Appalachian Trail, as they call it in Floyd these days, written on the landscape and written into the memories of people who have a powerful sense of place and of their own history. So, while the original section of the Appalachian Trail in Southwestern Virginia has disappeared from the official narrative of the trail, it survives nonetheless.

Historians and anthropologists have long understood that traces of the past exert a powerful influence on the present, providing the raw material for stories that people tell about themselves, about their communities and about their intended futures. Southwestern Virginia is a place where history permeates the ways that longtime residents understand and organize their world. Many of those residents in places like Floyd, Comer's Creek, Grant, Meadows of Dan or Fancy Gap trace their families' residence in the southern uplands to land grants made after the Revolutionary War, while others remember that their ancestors arrived with the factories built along the New River around the turn of the century. Some remember that their families were freed from slavery after the Civil War, and an even smaller number remember that their ancestors lived there for centuries before the white settlers came to take up those land grants and push the indigenous communities out. But even recent arrivals to the region feel the weight of history, feel its presence and retell stories of events from one hundred or two hundred years ago as if they happened just a few years back. The music written and played here on the fiddle, the banjo, the dobro, the dulcimer, the mandolin and the guitar harks back to a time when new immigrants to the region brought ballads of sorrow and loss, songs of joy and hymns of grace and forgiveness and suffering.

Their lives are shaped by the mountains, by the weather that blows down from the peaks or upslope from the Piedmont below. The land is almost never flat nor the roads straight. Weeks are ordered by the rhythms of work and of church and still, in few places, the factory whistle. They are fully connected to the world but have a sense of being separate at the same time. They remember the way big corporations based somewhere else treated them as places for extraction, resources to be used, people to be taken advantage of. They worry that all that money being promised to Amazon up in Northern Virginia is being taken from the people of the New River Valley. They wonder what's going to happen next that will bring jobs and convince the young people to stay. Some of the old home places have been abandoned, but others are still where the family gathers for dinner or lunch on Sunday.

Coles Knob, Floyd County, Virginia, in 2018. *Author's collection.*

Some residents of the region have arrived much more recently, in this lifetime, and have no people buried here and worry less about the past. They came to live in one of the many intentional communities that sprouted up beginning in the 1960s. They came to retire from the hustle of the cities. They came to live sustainable lives. Even though they might be "northern people" or "city people" or from "down the mountain," those very recent arrivals are part of the landscape of Southwestern Virginia as well. But the history is not theirs. It's not alive for them the way it is for the folks who can tell you about something that happened in 1912 as though it happened last month. They aren't shaped by that history. They're interested in it, the way most people are vaguely interested in the history of the places they live now, but it isn't written on their bones. Even so, they see the traces of the Appalachian Trail here or there and interpret those traces of the past from their own frames of reference.

The organization of this book is not what you might expect in an "Appalachian Trail history." There is a linear narrative of the trail's creation and demise in this part of Southwestern Virginia from 1930 to 1952, and so those who just want to know what happened back then will find what they were hoping for. But you won't find it in neatly ordered chapters that lay out the events of 1930 and then of 1931 and then of 1932 and so on. History isn't really like that, no matter how your high school teacher outlined it on the board. History is a mess, a mess that slides back and forth across the decades and the centuries, being written and rewritten, fought over, agreed on and rewritten again when new doors open or new evidence floats to the surface. And so, like history, this book is built on a foundation of sequential events but uses them to examine the past and the present simultaneously, because only if we examine both—past and present at the same time—can we truly understand the history of Virginia's Lost Appalachian Trail.

FIRST STEPS

The pleasure of walking, or rather of hiking, comes from the utter sense of freedom incident to getting away from crowded cities and equally crowded highways, from escaping the daily grind over desk or bench, in office, school, or shop, and discovering the beauties and peace of the forest primeval.
—*Roy Ozmer, "Do You Want to Walk 2,000 Miles?"*
Atlanta Constitution, *1928*

On August 1, 1930, in Virginia's Peaks of Otter, a man from Georgia checked out of his room at the Hotel Mons and started walking south. His name was Roy Ozmer. If anyone asked him what he was doing, he would have told them that he was a trail scout for an organization up in Washington, D.C., called the Appalachian Trail Conference. Without a doubt, no one at the hotel would had heard of that organization, although there was a very outside chance they might have heard of the "Appalachian Trail." Ozmer, a mountain man with the soul of a poet, made friends easily, even if he did prefer a life of solitude in the mountains. He was always happy to strike up a conversation with anyone he met, so he just might have chatted with other guests at the hotel. If any of them had talked with him, he would have explained that the trail he was there to scout went north from the Peaks of Otter all the way to Maine and that when he was done investigating the route south to the Tennessee line, it would go all the way to Georgia. He would have told them that his plan was to mark out one of the last unmarked sections of the Appalachian Trail, thus completing the first phase of the grand project Benton MacKaye had first dreamed up in 1921.

Roy Ozmer camping on the Appalachian Trail, 1930s. *Appalachian Trail Conservancy Archives.*

Ozmer knew what he was about, as he'd already scouted the Georgia section of the trail mostly by himself the year before. Once he'd scouted the trail all the way to the Georgia/North Carolina line, he had gone back to the trail's southern terminus on Mount Oglethorpe in Georgia (which he selected over the objections of hikers in Tennessee who wanted the terminus closer to Knoxville), with the intention of hiking all the way to Mount Katahdin in Maine before the snow began to fall. That first known attempt at a thru hike of the Appalachian Trail—a thru hike over a trail that wasn't even yet complete—ended when Ozmer took a bad fall in Tennessee and injured his back so severely that he had to quit and go home. But the lure of the trail called him on for decades.

If Ozmer did discuss his plans with the other guests at the Hotel Mons, they probably would have thought he was crazy. Hike two thousand miles from Georgia to Maine? What an idea. But Ozmer was entranced with the southern forests and by the idea that animated MacKaye's proposal for the AT, and he believed he was the man to make it happen in the South. "At the time I first became interested in the [AT] movement it was impossible to find anyone south of Washington who knew whether the Appalachian Trail was liquid or solid," he wrote in an account of his attempted thru hike. The future trail would offer anyone with a minimum of outdoor skill the chance to "strike a section of a well-marked trail which will lead him deep into the vast seclusion of the true wilderness, where sounds not the blatant bawl of a 'klaxon'; nor the voices of giddy flappers, escorted by the 'Knights of the Over-Stuffed Sofa!'" he wrote. With the same missionary zeal evinced by other builders of the Appalachian Trail, Ozmer hoped that "those who travel along the trail may have at least a fraction of the thrills, the intense pleasure and the sense of a closeness to the pulsing heart of nature, which has been my lot to experience."

That August morning in 1930, though, Ozmer was no missionary. Instead, he was a puzzling sight. He wasn't a large man—in fact, he was kind of small, wiry really, and he favored a tall, wide-brimmed hat when he hiked. Not quite a cowboy hat, but close. It wouldn't have been the hat, though, that caught people's eye. Instead, it would have been the large wheel attached to a stick that he was pushing in front of him. It was a measuring wheel, he would have explained if they asked. He needed the wheel to keep accurate measurements of the route because the man he worked for up in Washington, a government lawyer named Myron Avery, was a stickler for accuracy when it came to measuring trails, naming mountains or really everything. In fact, calling Avery a stickler doesn't come close to how exacting he was. Ozmer knew this because he'd worked for Avery before, and he knew that his boss was difficult to satisfy. Very difficult. Almost impossible, to be honest about it. So that morning at the gate of the hotel, he made sure that he set the ticker on the measuring wheel to 0.0 before he started walking south along the road, pushing that wheel along in front of him.

It was hot that day, even for Central Virginia in August. In fact, it had been unusually hot the whole month of July and would stay that way all of August. In that heat, it must have been hard to leave the Hotel Mons, with its wide shady veranda stretching from one end of the building to the other and its excellent meals. Even in 1930, with the economy already a mess, people still came up to the Mons to spend the night, hike up and down the Peaks of Otter and, after a day of healthy exertion, return to the hotel, where they could sit down with the other guests for family-style dinner— fried chicken, mashed potatoes, green beans and fresh fruit pie for dessert. But things being as they were after the stock market crash, fewer people came up the mountain than they did when the place first opened a decade earlier, and it wouldn't be much longer before the hotel failed and was sold to the National Park Service, which then tore it down during the war. That was all in the future though. Hot day or not, Ozmer had a job to do and a boss who expected results, so he left the shade in the hotel's front yard,

Hotel Mons in 1937. *Author's collection.*

stepped onto Virginia Highway 43, still a dirt road in 1930, and pointed his measuring wheel south.

By the time Ozmer started walking down Highway 43, the Appalachian Trail project, first proposed by the regional planner and sometime federal forester Benton MacKaye in 1921, was well underway, but only after a series of fits and starts. MacKaye's proposal, published as an essay in the *Journal of the American Institute of Architects* in 1921, called for the creation of something much more than just a path through the mountains of the East. MacKaye, an active Socialist with very progressive views about both environmental matters and the need for American workers to live healthier lives, wanted his future trail to be the nexus of a series of not-for-profit volunteer projects that would help create "a socialized outdoor life for the workers of the nation." He also believed that his proposed trail would help cure American society of the problems created by capitalism, industrial exploitation of the environment and rapid technological change. The Appalachian Trail would be, he hoped, a place where people could find solutions to "the problem of living" caused by the First World War, economic dislocation and the ever-increasing stresses of urban society. Because this trail was to be built for the people who toiled in the great cities of the Eastern Seaboard, it should be located as close to those cities as possible along the easternmost ridges of the Appalachian mountains and should include a series of "shelter camps" that would be "at convenient distances so as to allow a comfortable day's walk between each."

MacKaye's back-to-nature utopianism also included the future development of what he called "community camps" that would not be "real estate ventures" but rather "self-owned" communities that would remain small and would promote various non-industrial uses of nature—recreation, recuperation, scientific investigation and even outdoor education programs. He also hoped that one day "food and farm camps" would develop near the proposed trail that could supply the nutritional needs of those in the community camps and hikers in the wilderness. These, too, would be cooperative ventures that provided opportunities for urban dwellers to return to the land. Today, Floyd County is filled with such communities—eco-villages, intentional communities, ashrams—where people go for a few days, a few weeks or maybe the rest of their lives, to get away from the same stresses and strains that MacKaye felt were destroying the health and peace of the people in America's cities. Of course, these new communities aren't connected to the trail's history at all, but a number of the residents of those places have contacted me to get more information on "the old trail" because they want to hike its route, to use it for bicycle touring or to just show it to friends.

To his surprise and immense gratification, his proposal for a long-distance hiking trail along the spine of the Appalachians found a ready audience among the hiking community in the Northeast. Two months after his essay appeared, MacKaye spoke to the New England Trail Conference about his vision and received strong positive feedback. Leaders of this organization had already been working on ideas to link their various trail networks in New England and were excited by MacKaye's much larger vision for a trail network extending far to the south. Where MacKaye's vision differed from theirs, however, was in the matter of ideology. MacKaye saw his Appalachian Trail as a project in social transformation, while for many in the hiking community, a trail was nothing more than a recreational resource—a place to get away for a few hours, a few days or perhaps a few weeks. This difference in outlook and long-term goals put MacKaye at odds with those who began to work to realize his proposal. He wanted something grand that would change America for the better. They wanted a *really long trail* that they and other hikers could walk on, and before long, the leaders of these trail clubs had taken over the project and all but pushed MacKaye to the margins.

But that was all in the future. In the mid-1920s, MacKaye and several like-minded conservationists and hiking club members managed to organize a meeting of what MacKaye decided to call the Appalachian Trail Conference in Washington, D.C. The original members of the ATC represented a professionally diverse coalition of people (albeit all white men), including

Judge Arthur Perkins in 1927.
Appalachian Trail Conservancy Archives.

government officials like Director of the National Park Service Stephen Mather and representatives of trail clubs in the Northeast, like the venerable Appalachian Mountain Club (AMC) and the more recent but still impressive Green Mountain Club, whose members were in the process of completing the last links of their Long Trail from the Canadian border all the way down to the Vermont/Massachusetts line. Oddly, or perhaps presciently, the leaders of the new Conference didn't select MacKaye as one of their leaders, even though the whole thing was his idea and he was the one who had called them together in the first place. They were all men of action, doers, and MacKaye was a dreamer, a visionary who at times came off as a bit of a flake, so it's no surprise, really, that they politely but firmly set him to the side, casting him in the role of their Nestor but giving him no particular authority over anything.

That authority they gave instead to Arthur Perkins, a longtime AMC member, avid outdoorsman and conservationist and a recently retired judge living in Connecticut. Just as important as his love of the outdoors and his devotion to hiking was the fact that Perkins had money. The original incarnation of the ATC had no budget of its own, so it was Perkins who paid for much of the early work on the creation of the Appalachian Trail, including the $110 it took to fund Ozmer's scouting expedition in the summer of 1930. Perkins was a boisterous, affable man who had little difficulty convincing the various outdoor clubs north of the Susquehanna River to connect their trail systems to one another. Although there was plenty of work to do to make those trails connect, at least in the Northeast, there was something there to work with. In fact, compared to the work that had to be done south of the Susquehanna, connecting those existing trails was pretty easy.

When the trail planners at the ATC hauled out their maps of Vermont and New Hampshire, they saw lots of good trails already marked out with little dotted lines made by the AMC or the Green Mountain Club. In other places like New York and Pennsylvania, there were some shorter trails on the maps or old abandoned dirt roads—or at least what seemed like abandoned roads to the lawyers, engineers and their friends living in cities like Boston,

New York, Philadelphia and Washington. With a little creative use of colored pencils, those old roads and bits of existing trails could be connected into something like a continuous trail route. Once they'd plotted out that part of the route, the trail planners moved on to more difficult problems—like Maine; like the "Lost Province" of Western North Carolina and the bits of East Tennessee that clung to the steep slopes of the Smokies, the Nantahalas and the Unakas; like North Georgia, where nothing approximating a hiking trail existed in the northeastern corner of the state; and most of all, like the high mountain plateau of Southwestern Virginia, where none of them had ever been and for which there weren't even good maps to work with.

There were a lot of scientific and rational ways that the leaders at the ATC could have approached the planning, the cutting and the blazing of a trail in all those harder-to-get to places. They were, after all, rational men. Men of science. Members of the bar. Government men. But scientific and rational ways of doing things can take a long time, and these were also men in a hurry. They had a vision—a vision of a trail that started in Georgia and ended in Maine—and they were doers. They wanted their trail *done*, not so they or anyone else could hike from Georgia to Maine or from Maine to Georgia in one year—that crazy notion never entered their minds, or if it did, they didn't talk about it out loud. They wanted to be able to take their colored pencils and connect all those states and all those trails into a complete and continuous line, with no gaps at all, and to then put the local trail clubs that existed, or were in the process of being created, to work on cutting, leveling, side hill cribbing and eventually smoothing out the trail along the route they'd marked. When the work was done, they would know that they had done something audacious, something big, something that no one else had ever done, something they could be proud of.

Of all those doers, Myron Avery was the one who was pushing the hardest to connect all those lines. When the whole thing started, Avery wasn't in charge of anything other than one of the local trail clubs—the Potomac Appalachian Trail Club, which he and several friends created in Washington, D.C., in 1927. A young lawyer from hardscrabble Lubec, Maine, and an avid hiker and outdoor writer, Avery had the drive and energy level of two or maybe three grown men. At the meeting creating the PATC, Avery's friends recognized that there really wasn't anyone else who was better suited to be in charge of their club and so selected him as their first president. Within a few weeks, PATC members began hacking their way through the forests of Northern Virginia between Ashby Gap and Manassas Gap, laying down the oldest bit of the Appalachian Trail in the state that now encompasses

Myron Avery on the Appalachian Trail with his measuring wheel in 1935. *Appalachian Trail Conservancy Archives.*

a quarter of the trail's current length. Avery and his PATC collaborators worked like demons almost every weekend to extend their segment of the trail north and south, and before long, it was apparent to almost everyone involved with the ATC that Avery was the kind of leader they needed to bring the project to completion. Believing that he was the man to get it done was not the same thing as liking him, because Avery could be a very dislikable person. He was curt, demanding, sometimes insulting, easily drawn into arguments over the smallest things, always in a hurry and prone to perceive personal insults where none was intended or really even existed. But he got things done. No one could deny that. Given the challenges of building the Appalachian Trail south of the Susquehanna River, Avery just seemed like the logical choice to lead the charge, and he was more than happy to take that leading role. From his perch as PATC president, Avery increasingly assumed the day-to-day leadership of all efforts south of the Susquehanna, and Perkins, who by then was experiencing some serious health problems, seems to have been more than happy to let Avery do just that.

Avery's plan for the southern half of the trail had two parts. The first was to encourage the establishment of a series of trail maintaining clubs to the south of Charlottesville, Virginia (the southern limit of PATC's territory), so that once the trail was plotted and blazed, those local clubs could take over the difficult and sweaty work of trail building and trail maintenance. To that end, Avery encouraged the creation of two of the oldest Appalachian Trail maintaining clubs: the Natural Bridge Appalachian Trail Club in Lynchburg, Virginia, and the Roanoke Appalachian Trail Club farther south. He also gave similar encouragement to the founding of the Georgia Appalachian Trail Club and helped recruit the already existing Smoky Mountains Hiking Club and the Carolina Mountain Club to the Appalachian Trail project. The second part of his plan was to quickly, and quietly, get the trail blazed along lines that *he* approved before anyone from those trail clubs could choose the route for the new trail.

To achieve his goals, Avery tracked down a small group of men who would do his bidding in those less than accessible mountains and who would find a route for the trail. In Georgia, it was Arthur Woody, the pistol-toting "Barefoot Ranger," and a young forester named Roy Ozmer. In North Carolina and Tennessee, it was Paul Fink, who helped found the ATC back in 1925, and a Japanese American photographer named George Masa, who ran a little photography studio in Asheville and had the uncanny ability to walk up onto a mountain family's front porch, way up in a hollow, and in his broken English introduce himself and find out just about everything about the hills and hollows where they lived. In Maine, it was Walter Greene, a Broadway actor who loved nothing better than chopping his way through the all but impenetrable spruce groves of the northeast forests with a hand axe. And in Southwestern Virginia, it was Roy Ozmer once again, whom Avery charged with finding a route for the trail. Avery wasn't the kind of

Measuring the Appalachian Trail with Myron Avery in 1940. *Roanoke Appalachian Trail Club Archives.*

leader who could sit still up in Washington while his intrepid representatives bushwhacked their way forward. He was constantly out in the mountains with them, pushing his measuring wheel everywhere he went. What must the mountain folks he met have made of that wheel?

Of all the places that the trail had to be laid out, only Maine and Southwestern Virginia posed really significant problems. North Georgia, Western North Carolina and East Tennessee weren't easy, but they were more or less known. Avery was from Maine and had hiked extensively in the Katahdin region—he had even written a book on the mountain—and so had a good feel for what could and could not be accomplished east of the New Hampshire line. He knew, for instance, that there were hunting and fishing camps all over Central Maine, and so he told Walter Greene to find ways to link those places together and, eventually, create a route that ran from the New Hampshire line all the way to Katahdin. Because the reports he received from Greene were filled with names and places he knew, he worried a lot less about Maine. Southwestern Virginia, though, was much more of a problem for Avery because not only did he not know the region at all, but it also wasn't even properly mapped by the government. In some cases, the most recent government topographic maps dated from the 1880s or even as far back as the Civil War. Forty- or even sixty-year-old maps were simply not good enough to satisfy Avery's need for exactitude.

Myron Avery's personal nightmare scenario, one that he did everything in his power to avoid, was for the members of local trail clubs to scout out routes for the Appalachian Trail, routes that he, Myron Avery, had not approved in advance. To keep the local clubs at bay, Avery relied on agents of his own desire like Ozmer and Greene to scout routes for him so he could forestall others from laying down their own route for the trail. Instead, he would give the club leaders maps with the trail already marked out and say, "That's where the trail will go." By early 1930, Avery was feeling pressure about the Southwestern Virginia route, which, along with Maine, was the last segment of the trail that no one had mapped. Perkins had been asking him what was happening south of Roanoke, had already been hearing from trail enthusiasts in the region and had reached out to Paul Fink in Tennessee for advice on where to route the trail south of Roanoke. "It is quite out of the question to turn such a group loose and tell them to locate a trail," Avery wrote to Ozmer about local trail clubs in early July. "What we want to do is have an exact location worked out and let [them] put markers, etc. on this previously determined route." By then, Avery knew that two men from the southern plateau—Shirley L. Cole, the county agent in Floyd County south of Roanoke, and Donald Campbell of Mount Airy, North Carolina—had already scouted a possible route from Roanoke to Blowing Rock, North Carolina, and had sent a report to Perkins urging him to choose their proposed option. To forestall those advocates for the trail, Avery urged Ozmer to hit the road once more on his behalf and to mark out a route before anyone else did. After his failed thru hike attempt the year before, Ozmer was, in his words, "rearing to go," and told Avery that he could be on the job as early as late July.

Money had to be found for Ozmer's scouting trip, so Avery turned once again to Judge Perkins, who dutifully wired the money to Ozmer. And so, on August 1, the man from Georgia in his high almost-cowboy hat headed south into the heat of a Central Virginia summer. That first day, he stayed on the main road, known in those days as the Bedford-Buchanan Pike, for just under seven miles before turning off into the forest on one of the many "old faint wagon road[s]" and "dim trail[s]" that he would utilize in that initial foray off the main line of the Blue Ridge Mountains and south along the Great Escarpment of Southwestern Virginia. The most famous of the old roads Ozmer would make use of was known as the "Ridge Road." This mostly dirt track wound its way along the edge of the escarpment from Salem to Fisher's Peak just across the North Carolina border and from there south toward South Carolina. In 1930, the Ridge Road wasn't much of a road any longer, although it had once been an important commercial artery. Later that year, Myron Avery decided to check up on the route Ozmer had proposed and described it as muddy and "just barely passable for cars." But that road had quite a history. Before people in that part of Virginia started calling it the Ridge Road, it was sometimes known as the Wagon Road or just the road to Philadelphia. More than one hundred years earlier, when the railroads hadn't yet stolen all the cartage, that road along the edge of the Blue Ridge ran from Philadelphia all the way down into the Carolinas and has been described by some historians as the busiest road in colonial America and in the early republic. Teams of mules pulled wagons over the corduroy and through the mud, bringing raw materials and processed goods north or finished products, especially tools and agricultural implements, south. The railroads killed off what some historians call the "Great Wagon Road," but in 1930, it was still there, sometimes passable by car, sometimes not, but very available to Roy Ozmer.

Ozmer likely didn't know it, but the Ridge Road was far older than the founding of the British colonies in America. Before Europeans arrived in Southwestern Virginia, the Iroquois and the Cherokee had laid down an intricate network of trails that they used for commerce, for war, for reinforcing their spiritual connection to the land and to visit neighboring villages and clans. Indigenous trail makers preferred ridgeline trails because they generally offered paths of least resistance—fewer streams to cross and less undergrowth to bash through. European settlers made extensive use of the preexisting indigenous trail network, and the Ridge Road Ozmer selected was just one example of how useful a ridgeline road could be to modern trail builders. The Cherokee laid out the route for the sake of efficiency or to access holy places, the settlers used that path because it satisfied their need for an easier route north or south and Ozmer used it because it was available and because it often offered excellent views of the Piedmont below. Eventually, the planners of the Blue Ridge Parkway chose Ozmer's route for many of the same reasons, but by the time the Appalachian Trail came to the region, the many layers of indigenous history underneath the Ridge Road were long forgotten, or if they were remembered, those memories did not find their way into any contemporary description of the Appalachian Trail I have found.

Before he got to the Ridge Road, however, Ozmer had to swing well south of Roanoke and Salem. To do that, he followed the ridgeline from the Peaks of Otter until he was just north of Vinton, at which point he cut almost due south to pick up the ridgeline on the south side of the city of Roanoke. From there, Ozmer continued to Airpoint and eventually on toward Adney Gap, where he picked up the Ridge Road after more than sixty-five miles had ticked off on his measuring wheel. At this point, Ozmer did his best to walk what he called the "water divide," a plan that kept him as close to the eastern edge of the escarpment as possible. That water divide was the point of separation between the Roanoke River watershed and the New River watershed, with the creeks on his left flowing into the Atlantic and those on his right flowing first north into West Virginia and then eventually into the Mississippi and the Gulf of Mexico. When he wasn't on the Ridge Road, Ozmer was making liberal use of "dim trails," "very faint trails," "faint road[s]" or "dim roads" to find a path for the AT. In other words, Roy Ozmer was not blazing a trail in the mountains when he scouted a route for the Appalachian Trail in Southwestern Virginia. He was just trying to find a way to route the trail with the most interesting geographic features while making it possible for hikers to find their way without too much difficulty. As a result, the Appalachian Trail in Southwestern Virginia east of the New River, right from the start, was largely a "road trail," one that relied heavily on current and abandoned roads as the path through the forests and fields of the great plateau. It's hard to remember now, but hundreds and hundreds of miles of the original Appalachian Trail were "road trails." It wasn't until the 1980s that almost all of that road walking had been eliminated for good.

Ozmer's generally prodigious route-finding skills failed him once he made his way south from Sling's Gap. His report to the ATC, written at the conclusion of his foray from the Peaks of Otter, shows just how frustrated he was that August:

> *I found it utterly impossible, despite a broad experience in such work, to locate the logical route for the Trail in the regions between Sling's Gap and Galax. In order to know the region well enough to definitely locate the trail, it would be necessary that a stranger spend not less than six months in that section.... The usual thing encountered in the Appalachian mountains is a series of high, well-defined ridges leading in general from n.e. to s.w. In this section, all this is changed. The entire region between the points mentioned is merely a high plateau or tableland, rising gently from the w. and reaching its climax on the water divide of the Blue Ridge...there are no sharp, well-defined ridges, prominent peaks, standing above the plateau, with the exception of Buffalo Mt. in Floyd County.*

Ozmer spent four days wandering along the rim of the escarpment south of Sling's Gap before finally throwing in the towel and calling for reinforcements, thereby doing the very thing Avery had wanted to avoid in the first place—let local trail enthusiasts who were not under Avery's control decide where the trail should go. That's why he had hired Ozmer in the first place. But Ozmer needed help, so he turned to Shirley Cole in Floyd, Virginia, the same Shirley Cole who had written to Judge Perkins earlier in the year proposing a route for the trail from Blowing Rock, North Carolina, to Salem, Virginia. The same Shirley Cole who had come to the annual meeting of the ATC earlier that year at Skyland Lodge in the Shenandoahs and given a formal presentation about possible routes for the Appalachian Trail in Southwestern Virginia. The same Shirley Cole whom Avery had been trying to forestall by hiring Ozmer. Cole wasn't the only "local enthusiast" Ozmer had spoken to during his blundering about south of Roanoke, but it was likely because he had met Cole at the Skyland Conference earlier in the year that he turned to the county agent from Floyd. After a day of discussing the matter at Cole's home, the two men set off on a driving tour that completely changed Ozmer's view of this part of Southwestern Virginia:

> *When I first left the high, yet dull and uninteresting water divide, I was skeptical of anything of the scenic value reputed to be found in the region. After having spend [sic] more than a week traversing the seventy miles of the rim, both alone and then later with the excellent guidance of Mr. Cole, I came away an enthusiast myself. The region is truly different and unique among the eastern mountains, so far as my knowledge extends.*

What exactly was it that impressed Ozmer so much? After all, he'd spent most of his life hiking in the mountains of Georgia, East Tennessee and Western North Carolina, where he'd seen pretty much the best the Southern Appalachians have to offer—the Great Smoky Mountains, the Unakas, the great balds along the North Carolina/Tennessee line, the view from Blood Mountain in Georgia and more. What was so unique, so different about the mountains he now found himself in as he tramped around with Shirley Cole?

The mountains there *were* different. Just south of Roanoke, the great eastern ridge of the Appalachian Range divides, with one branch angling in a more or less southwestern direction toward Wytheville, down into the Iron Mountain Range and eventually to the Unakas of East Tennessee and Western North Carolina. The other branch of those mountains runs almost due south to the North Carolina border at Fisher's Peak, where it then bends southwest toward Blowing Rock, North Carolina, eventually reuniting with the northern branch of the ridgeline. Between those two arms of the Appalachians lies a vast upland plateau where mountain summits rise above 5,000 feet and even the wind gaps top out above 2,500 feet. That plateau, a place that geologists call the Blue Ridge Escarpment, is visible from out in the Virginia and North Carolina Piedmont as a vast blue wall rearing up from the rolling lands below. Rising more than 2,000 feet in places, what seems like a wall from a distance, is really a network of gorges, small stream valleys, cliffs and gentler slopes that provide both a geological and a biological dividing line between the Piedmont and the peaks of the Appalachians.

In between that escarpment and the peaks is a land all its own. Driving or walking around the area, it's difficult to realize that you are already more than 2,500 feet above sea level because the lands around you can seem as gentle as the Piedmont just a few miles to the east. The rolling farmlands are filled with Black Angus cattle or are covered in pumpkins, and on the slopes, Christmas trees planted in neat lines await shipment to the urban markets to the east. The land is dotted with ramshackle barns that seem ready to collapse at a moment's notice, tiny churches made with white clapboard or stone, old motels from a tourist era long past and big new farm houses or vacation homes that speak to the arrival of new money in the region. But the edge of the escarpment is wild, with treacherous roads that wind crazily down into gorges, sudden cascades appearing seemingly from nowhere and huge cliffs, some of them made entirely of quartz crystals, falling away toward the Piedmont below. The Ridge Road ran mostly along the boundary between this wild land and the rolling farmlands beyond, and it was routing the trail along this boundary between wild and tame that called out to Ozmer.

One of the most unique features of this region, and one that Ozmer noted right away, is that the great wall of the Blue Ridge in Southwestern Virginia is a watershed boundary. As he learned while trying to find a path south from Sling's Gap, the rivers and streams that drain Southwestern Virginia's great upland plateau are confused and confusing. On the eastern face of the escarpment, water flows into the Roanoke River basin and thus, eventually, into Albemarle-Pamlico Sound in North Carolina. When colonial settlers first began to settle the lowlands near the escarpment, that meant that their goods could not easily be shipped to English markets because they would have to travel overland to get to the main colonial ports on the Chesapeake Bay. This reality limited settlement and remained a problem right up to the time when railroads, and then roads, finally made their way into the region, contributing to the long-term semi-isolation of the farms and towns on the plateau. Goods produced on the plateau could also travel along the New River, perhaps the oldest river in North America, but the New River flows north, then west to the Ohio River and then to the Mississippi, finally reaching the Gulf of Mexico at New Orleans, a trip far too long to make good economic sense. And so, white settlers in the region were doomed from the start to rely on local trade. Only when the railroads finally arrived around 1900 did the great plateau of Southwestern Virginia become more fully integrated into the national economy. For trail planners like Ozmer and Avery, though, the limits local geography placed on economic development were a plus, as it meant that even though much of their hike east of the New River would be along old roads, hikers would be passing through largely undeveloped or underdeveloped regions of the state and so would be largely untroubled by cars, trucks and trains.

Having been convinced both of the scenic value of locating the Appalachian Trail along the eastern rim of the Great Escarpment, and of Shirley Cole's fitness to be the person leading the charge in that part of the state, Ozmer concluded his report with an enthusiastic recommendation that Cole be put in charge of the route from Sling's Gap to Galax and then south and west from Galax toward Damascus. Cole had convinced Ozmer that there were many others in the region just as enthusiastic about the Appalachian Trail and that he (Cole) had already organized several local Appalachian Trail clubs—in Floyd, in Meadows of Dan and in Galax—that would provide the labor for marking, cutting, grading and eventually maintaining the trail in that part of the state and that they would build half a dozen trailside shelters along the lines of those already being constructed in Northern Virginia and elsewhere along the trail.

Whether Avery was happy about this recommendation or not is unknown. What we do know is that he signed off on Ozmer's recommendation and, with typical Avery-esque enthusiasm and energy, put his Southwestern Virginia trail eggs into Shirley Cole's basket. In a letter to Cole, just after receiving Ozmer's report in early September, Avery wrote that he was accepting Ozmer's view of the route for the trail in Southwestern Virginia and that "you be authorized to proceed with the development of the trail as thus surveyed." Having thrown his lot in with Cole, Avery was clearly concerned that Cole might have taken it amiss that Avery had sent Ozmer to scout out routes for the trail after Cole and his friend Campbell had already proposed a route to Judge Perkins. In his letter authorizing Cole to get to work, Avery explained that he never would have routed the trail in any way that wasn't acceptable to Cole and Campbell. With no hint

The Galax Gang at Lovers Leap in 1930. *Potomac Appalachian Trail Club Archives.*

of disingenuousness, Avery explained that his whole reason for sending Ozmer into their part of the state was so that he (Avery) would be in a strong position to support their original recommendation. Avery was also quick to praise Ozmer to the now ailing Perkins, adding a marginal note to the copy of his letter to Cole, saying that Ozmer had done "a remarkable job. Has solved the problem." Avery wasn't shy, however, in explaining to the ATC Executive Committee that despite Cole's presentation at the Skyland Conference, "We were rather afraid to have a disconnected group undertake the location of the trail in Southwestern Virginia, lest it would not connect with the trail route at either end."

But having read Ozmer's report, likely especially the part where Ozmer said it would have taken him six months or longer to find the best route for the trail in Southwestern Virginia, Avery was at pains to reassure the Executive Committee that Cole was indeed the person to whom it should entrust this section of the trail. And trust Cole the committee did. On September 23, Avery was able to write back to Cole to let him know that the ATC Executive Committee had agreed to name him the ATC's authorized representative in Southwestern Virginia and that he and his trail enthusiasts should get to work on the Appalachian Trail in their area right away.

Avery, being Avery, couldn't leave things there. He had to get down to Southwestern Virginia himself to eyeball Cole and to see at least a little bit of the region he had called "our terra incognita." Two weeks after giving

Cole the go-ahead, Avery was in Floyd for a meeting with Cole and his collaborators who took him for a hike up Pumpkin Stem Knob, the first of several trips Avery would take to Southwestern Virginia to survey and, at least on one trip, to help build a section of the trail in the region. Following that first visit by the head honcho of the ATC, Cole went to work both on the trail that had been entrusted to him and, without Avery's formal approval, formed a Southwestern Virginia Appalachian Trail Club. Cole hoped to form associated clubs in half a dozen towns on the Southwestern Virginia plateau, news that must have given Avery a bad case of the shakes because he was in the middle of overseeing the creation of Appalachian Trail maintaining clubs in both Roanoke and Lynchburg that would be so closely modeled on the PATC that they essentially adopted the PATC constitution as written. Cole was writing his own rules without asking for Avery's input.

Cole was a lot like Avery in that he "was always organizing things," according to his daughter Dorothy, who was 101 when I interviewed her. In addition to getting the Appalachian Trail underway in Southwestern Virginia, in his capacity as county agent, Cole organized a huge Fourth of July barbecue in the town of Floyd that was, Dorothy told me, the biggest such celebration in the town of Floyd, complete with a line of barbecue

The Cole brothers at their cabin on Cockram Ridge in 1932. *Appalachian Trail Conservancy Archives.*

pits and a truck filled with fiddlers. "Everybody was so excited, everybody came," she said. Cole had been raised on the slopes of Coles Knob, just west of the town of Check in Floyd County. After graduating from the Kelley School, a one-room schoolhouse now preserved by the Blue Ridge Parkway, Cole attended Virginia Tech, where he was a student in a one-year certificate program for high school graduates who intended to work in agriculture. This training helped him land a job as the county agent in Stafford County, Virginia, where his two daughters were born. From Stafford, he returned to Southwestern Virginia, first as the county agent for Patrick County and then finally as the county agent for his home place in Floyd. When it came to work on the Appalachian Trail, in addition to members of the local Appalachian Trail clubs he helped create, Cole would take groups of boys from the 4-H or the Future Farmers of America up into the mountains with him to mark, cut and level sections of the trail. According to Dorothy, "The trail was all he cared about. He thought there was nothing like the mountains and the woods in the summertime.…When he worked on the trail he would hang his hammock between two trees in the woods and would lay trail in the mountains all day. He had a cabin that he built up on Coles Knob. It had a stream running right through it. He called it his running water."

With characteristic enthusiasm and energy, Cole and his local partners set about marking the route south from the Roanoke area. So much of the trail east of the New River followed existing or abandoned roadbeds that it didn't take long for the route from the Peaks of Otter to Galax to take shape. By early 1931, the first hikers were trying out portions of the new trail route. Some of the early hikers came from the local area, but others came down from Roanoke, where the Roanoke Appalachian Trail Club had just formed. The work was hardly finished, though, when Shirley Cole disappeared from the story of the Lost Appalachian Trail. According to his daughter, her parents divorced in 1932, and Cole soon left town to find work in Texas, as many men did during the Great Depression. Dorothy and her sister went to live with their grandparents up on Coles Knob, and the Appalachian Trail was suddenly without its spiritual leader in Southwestern Virginia. Avery's solution was to ask the Roanoke Club to take over the trail south to the boundary between Floyd and Patrick Counties and to ask others to help him supervise the rest of the trail.

Roy Ozmer also dropped out of the history of the Appalachian Trail around the same time. His trail scouting days at an end, Ozmer went back to Georgia, where he got a job with the U.S. Forest Service working in the Cherokee National Forest. At some point after World War II, Ozmer migrated to Florida, taking up residence on Pelican Key near St. Petersburg, where he became locally famous as the "Hermit of Pelican Key." He lived alone on the key (in a national park) in a tiny ramshackle house he built from scrap lumber until the early 1960s, when a hurricane flattened his abode and washed away his large collection of books. By the late 1950s, Ozmer had become something of a tourist attraction, delighting visitors with stories of his life and surprising them with his wide knowledge of English literature. Shirley Cole made one more cameo appearance in the history of the Appalachian Trail. In 1958, he appeared in the mountains of Western North Carolina pushing a measuring wheel just like Myron Avery's. He was, he explained to a reporter for the Asheville newspaper, plotting out a better route for the trail from Roan Mountain to Standing Indian Mountain. No one from the local trail clubs had asked him to do it and no one from the ATC even knew he was there, but just as he did in Floyd County in 1929, Cole had hopes that the route he planned to propose would catch on. When asked why he, a retired man in his late sixties, would be wandering the mountains with a measuring wheel, with characteristic enthusiasm, Cole replied, "Someone has to start a thing like this."

BENT MOUNTAIN

At 16.9 m., just over crest, narrow road to right leads .5 m. to Bent Mountain (Camp Branch) Falls. These falls are probably the second highest in Virginia. This is a most rewarding trip.
—Guide to the Paths of the Blue Ridge, *1931*

In the fall of 2018, Bent Mountain, Virginia, was a very angry place. The Bent Mountain community, just across Poor Mountain from the cities of Roanoke and Salem, had become one of the epicenters of the struggle between local communities, the Appalachian Trail Conservancy, the Roanoke Appalachian Trail Club (RATC) and several local conservation and preservation groups on one side and the Mountain Valley Pipeline, backed by Virginia governor Ralph Northam and a coalition of business interests, on the other. Driving south from Roanoke that October, the road I was on running below the southeast slope of Poor Mountain was littered with "No Pipeline!" signs, some of them professionally done but most just spray painted on pieces of plywood and nailed up on telephone poles, on fence posts or sprouting up in people's front yards. "MVP is Stealing Land and Homes from Virginians!" and "Shame on Northam!" Anger over the pipeline's ragged scar on the landscape that was working its way slowly across the mountain and through the Bent Mountain community was palpable everywhere you looked.

People were mad that the state was taking their land for the benefit of an out-of-state energy company. They were mad that the economic benefits of the pipeline that the governor was touting would be felt not in Bent Mountain or anywhere else nearby but in northern West Virginia, where the shale gas that would travel through the pipeline was being fracked, or at the other end of the 303-mile-long pipe in Norfolk, where the gas was going to be converted to liquid natural gas and sold abroad. No one on Bent Mountain had been given an option as to whether the pipeline would run through their land, and no one was going to see a penny of that money unless they got a job working on the pipeline. If anyone did get such a job, it would be a surprise, because who in Bent Mountain, Virginia, knew how to build a natural

Mountain Valley Pipeline sign, Bent Mountain, Virginia, 2018. *Author's collection.*

gas pipeline? Most of all, though, people were mad because the company building the pipeline was tearing up the forests, orchards and farms that people had owned and tended for centuries with what seemed like no regard for the landscape itself. Lawsuits had been filed. Activists were blocking the route of the pipeline. Documentary filmmakers were wandering around asking questions. But the pipeline just crawled on.

When I drove through Bent Mountain looking for the old route of the Appalachian Trail, everyone I met was angry about the pipeline. Construction had paused because of an injunction from a judge, but it was impossible to miss the place where the construction crews had buzz-sawed their way south and east. On my right, a channel the width of a two-lane highway came down from the slopes of Poor Mountain to the road I was on. On my left, that gouge passed into and through a stand of trees, then farther down the slope and out of sight. It was an ugly thing, raw, inexorable and heartless. No wonder people were mad.

The Bent Mountain community is old by western Virginia standards, with some of those farms being torn up by the pipeline extending back into the middle of the eighteenth century, when white settlers began showing up and pushing the local Cherokee community farther west. Many of those early homesteads were little more than single-room log cabins in the forest, but those cabins were important because, once built, they gave the farmer the right to claim the land nearby as his own. Before long, however, those first settlers were themselves pushed aside by wealthier men whose claim to the land derived from grants given to them by Virginia's governors. Those men with names like Lewis, Coles and Terry established tobacco farms on the fertile land around Bent Mountain and brought the institution of slavery with them into the area. Compared to the large plantations of the Piedmont, the tobacco farms in the mountains were never as large or as profitable, and the number of enslaved men, women and children was correspondingly lower—perhaps in the dozens instead of the hundreds or thousands common elsewhere. But it is from these enslaved individuals, freed after the Civil War, that the African American presence in Montgomery, Floyd and Carroll Counties partly derives.

Those tobacco farmers had a difficult time bringing their product to market because their only option was an extension of the Ridge Road that they could use to get their goods up to Roanoke, in those days known as Big Lick due to the size of the salt deposits nearby. That connecting road was little more than a cleared route through the forest that mules and wagons could follow, but it made it possible for the farmers to bring their hogsheads of tobacco up and over the mountain and down to Roanoke or north to Lynchburg, where they could be put into bateaux and taken down the James River to the markets on the Chesapeake. Because geography was against tobacco farming, local residents turned to raising hogs, cutting and selling chestnut lumber, planting apple orchards and making moonshine or apple brandy that they sold in Roanoke and Salem.

Looking at my maps in 2018, I realized later that if the trail still came down over the mountain, hikers would have crossed that big ugly pipeline scar very close to the place where I had stopped to take a few pictures and to marvel at man's inhumanity toward the landscape if there is money to be made and carbon to be burned. Those hikers would have found the pipeline in Bent Mountain because in 1933, Myron Avery and the leadership of the newly formed Roanoke Appalachian Trail Club (RATC) had rerouted the trail up and over Poor Mountain, pulling it away from Roy Ozmer's original 1930 route that swung south of Roanoke. The route Ozmer had chosen got to the town of Bent Mountain via Adney Gap by looping south of Roanoke along the ridgeline that ran between the Peaks of Otter and Cahas Mountain, at 3,571 feet the tallest peak in Franklin County. Ozmer preferred the southern route because it provided such excellent views to the south and east, much like the view of Cahas that one gets from the Blue Ridge Parkway today.

Cahas Knob from the Blue Ridge Parkway in 2019. *Author's collection.*

But his meandering route south of Roanoke didn't last long. The RATC leadership hiked Ozmer's version of the trail in the winter of 1932 and were not nearly as impressed by the scenery as he had been. They decided that the trail required, as they put it in their first annual report, "a complete relocation"—just the first of many relocations of the trail between Roanoke and Damascus. With Myron Avery's permission, the RATC decided to shift the trail's route to "the more interesting route north of Roanoke," along the crest of Catawba Mountain, best known today as the location of Tinker Cliffs and McAfee Knob, with its grand views of the valley below, now including the scar on the landscape created by the Mountain Valley Pipeline. In the spring of 1932, Avery came to Roanoke and hiked along Tinker Mountain with RATC members, helping them mark the new route of the trail and giving them his personal seal of approval.

The route they selected across Catawba Mountain is the route the trail largely follows today, except for a brief period in the 1970s and early 1980s when landowners on the mountain managed to kick the trail off what they saw as their mountain in hopes of preventing it from becoming part of the national park being created after the passage of the National Scenic Trails Act in 1968. For a few years, hikers approaching Catawba Mountain

Hikers on McAfee Knob in 1935. *Appalachian Trail Conservancy Archives.*

from the north climbed the mountain and walked along the ridgeline that pointed almost due west, but rather than making a sharp left turn toward Tinker Cliffs, they had to scramble down the side of the mountain, hike across the valley made by Catawba Creek and then up North Mountain. Only then could they turn south again. That part of the hike was no fun for anyone, both because there was no water to be had anywhere along

North Mountain but also because if they looked east, they could see McAfee Knob but couldn't actually go there, thus missing out on the single most photographed spot on the entire AT. Only when they reached Highway 311 could they cut back east again toward Mason Cove, where they rejoined the trail's former route. But that was in the 1970s, and the trail did eventually return to McAfee Knob. In the 1930s, Avery and the RATC members had a different problem to solve. They needed to figure out where the trail should turn south toward Floyd County so it could reconnect with the route Ozmer had laid out two years earlier.

Avery and the RATC members chose a route that took hikers briefly along Highway 311 toward Mason Cove and then up a series of old dirt roads over the ridge south of Bradshaw. As they began to climb up and away from the highway, hikers passed several old abandoned forest cabins that subsequently were recommended as good camping sites. In the trail's early days, hikers often were advised to use abandoned farm houses, barns and sheds as places to camp all along the route of the Appalachian Trail from Georgia to Maine, but especially in the South, because there were very few trailside shelters except in Vermont, New Hampshire and Maine. The *Guide to the Paths of Blue Ridge* recommends "several fine campsites at abandoned mountaineers' cabins along this road," and "[t]o left in gap is abandoned house and spring" and "pass to the left an abandoned farmhouse with spring." Early long-distance hikers along the trail took full advantage of these old homesites as camping locations, often writing about having to shoo off rattlesnakes or copperheads that had claimed the homeplace as their own. If you hike over Poor Mountain today, down into the Bottom Creek Gorge Preserve owned by the Nature Conservancy, you can still hole up for the night in at least one old abandoned house in a place where the forest is closing in again, but that house feels a lot creepier than those old abandoned home places probably did in 1932. The one you pass today is filled with empty beer cans and smells of recent parties.

Hikers got to Bent Mountain from Bradshaw by first walking past Dixie Caverns along US 11 and from there to Glenvar, where they could cross the Roanoke River and head up and over first Poor Mountain and then up and onto Bent Mountain, a route that would have taken them right across the scar left behind by the construction of the Mountain Valley Pipeline. Like much of the trail in Southwestern Virginia, the option Avery and the RATC selected followed little-used or unused dirt roads past mountain orchards, small churches and the occasional farm. The route they chose over Poor Mountain on County Road 612 is still passable by car, but only just barely,

The Check Store in Check, Virginia, 2018. *Author's collection.*

and not at all in the winter. From the crest of the mountain, with what the first guidebooks described as "splendid views," hikers then descended to first Laurel and then Bottom Creek, where they joined another county road and headed off toward the small town of Check. Check was, and still is, home to the Check Store, where hikers could resupply and perhaps mail a letter from the local post office. From there, they could also arrange an overnight stay with a hot meal at the home of Cletus Reed and his wife, Clarice, in nearby Copper Hill.

One of the unique features of hiking the Appalachian Trail from Roanoke to Damascus in the 1930s and 1940s was the lack of trail shelters and thus the availability of accommodations from local residents. Today's Appalachian Trail hiker is very used to staying at one of the more than 250 trailside shelters or at one of the dozens of hiker hostels along the trail established specifically to provide a bed, a shower and a hot meal to hikers headed north and south along the trail. And, of course, there is the marvelous chain of huts maintained by the Appalachian Mountain Club that offer all these same conveniences. Mostly, though, hikers stay at or near one of the trail shelters built and cared for by the various trail clubs that maintain the Appalachian Trail. The building of that chain of shelters didn't get underway in a serious manner until 1937, and in Southwestern Virginia, there was never a serious effort by the ATC to build shelters along the trail.

Because most of the trail's route between Roanoke and New River ran along old abandoned or little-used roads, building such shelters wasn't particularly feasible, as any such shelter would sit right next to a road and would thus be open to use by anyone passing by, not just hikers. Although almost all of the trail west of the New River ran though Unaka (now Jefferson) National Forest, no shelters were built there either, although today there are several along that old route, all built after the Appalachian Trail moved and the abandoned trail became the Iron Mountain Trail. The reason no shelters were built in the Unaka National Forest was simply the result of a lack of manpower. No

Ma Sue Hall, Floyd, Virginia, circa 1920. *Old Church Gallery, Floyd, Virginia.*

trail club existed west of the New River in the 1930s or 1940s, and it was all the forest service could do to keep the trail marked and cleared. Building shelters for the few hikers who passed by would have been too much to ask.

Instead, hikers found accommodations at places like the home of Cletus and Clarice Reed near Check, with Susan Harris Hall in the town of Floyd, with John Barnard in Meadows of Dan or with Mrs. Erna Webb in Fancy Gap. Or they camped out in old abandoned farmhouses, barns or schools like the Kelley School, the Woods School or the Edwardsville School. The large number of abandoned schoolhouses available as campsites was the result of the spread of publicly funded schooling in this part of the state in the 1920s and the resulting failure of the one- and two-room schools that once upon a time had been the mainstay of the local educational system. By 1930, most of those schoolhouses were now just good places to camp under a roof for the night. Today, they're almost all gone.

But before they went to Check for a resupply and before they called Cletus and Clarice Reed for a room and a meal, hikers were strongly encouraged to take the "most rewarding" side trip to Bent Mountain Falls. Driving there today, in addition to the angry "No Pipeline!" signs, one sees every version of economic life in Southwestern Virginia. There are large prosperous farms, big new vacation homes, ramshackle mobile homes and dead cars rotting in fields between Highway 221 and the Bottom Creek Preserve parking area. First established in the late 1980s, the preserve now encompasses more than 1,600 acres of land in what was once one of the oldest communities in the Roanoke area. The families who still lived there in the 1930s when the Appalachian Trail arrived either farmed their own land, worked at nearby apple orchards or helped saw logs at the King brothers' steam-powered sawmill. On Sundays, they attended services at either the local Brethren church or the Christo Evangelical Wesleyan church. Both churches, with their quiet, simple style, still stand today along the road out of the Bottom, but neither hosts congregants any longer. Someone takes care of them, as the grass is cut and the paint isn't that old. But both have the look of places once important but now just cared for.

The trail passed right by the parking area for the preserve (along Route 637), and that parking area sits where hikers were urged to divert two-thirds of a mile up and over the ridge for the rewarding trip to see the falls. Avery's trail guide oversold the view, though, because Bent Mountain Falls, for all their height, are more of a cascade than a waterfall and are so tall and so located that they are very difficult to see except in the winter when the leaves are off the trees. The hike up the ridge from the parking lot follows and old abandoned roadbed through a dense growth of the sort of large rhododendron bushes endemic to this part of the state. On the left, the bushes front a small stream, and to the right, the ridge rises quickly toward

The King Brothers' Sawmill near Bent Mountain, Virginia, circa 1910. *Roanoke Public Library, Bent Mountain Collection.*

the summit through groves of locust and huge tulip poplars. Near the top of the ridge, another faded mountain road, the kind favored by the Appalachian Trail's creators, comes in from the right, and almost immediately another intersects from the left. These old roads, plus the bits of barbed wire nailed to old cedar fence posts and remnants of stacked stone walls, a partially tumbled chimney, are all that remain of the farms along the ridge that once belonged to families named King, Craighead, Funk and Hall who once farmed the flat area at the top of the mountain. Local folks used to call the Bottom Creek area "the roughs" because it was so difficult to get around, what with the steep slopes and tumbling streams. These days, the only rough part is the climb back up from the base of the falls.

The Bottom Creek Gorge area was also, briefly, the hideout of men trying to avoid service in the Civil War or who had deserted their units and hidden themselves away from Confederate government conscription gangs. The rough terrain and general inaccessibility of the gorge made it an ideal place for hiding out and a dangerous place for the men charged with rounding up the deserters and draft dodgers. One such attempt in 1863 resulted in the officer in charge, John. R. Peyton, being shot dead from his horse near the summit of Bent Mountain by three men who had fled their service in the Confederate army and who feared that Peyton would catch on to their status as deserters. One of the prosperous landowners on Bent Mountain shuddered at the poverty of the homes the deserters built. They were, she wrote, "the crudest of abodes. In their structure was neither an inch of metal, nor a piece of glass, nor any sawed timber. They were rock underpinned, clay daubed, with log pens, log sills and joists, supporting floors of split logs with the flat side up."

In 1932, though, no one was shooting at anyone on Bent Mountain, unless maybe the owner of a local whiskey or brandy still felt that his livelihood was being threatened by rivals or the local revenue agents. Then warning shots might have been fired. In fact, early tales of scouting and hiking the Appalachian Trail, including Ozmer's tale of marking out the trail in Georgia, Tennessee and North Carolina, are filled with stories of smelling smoke through the trees and being wary of running afoul of men making moonshine in the forest. Standard procedure for hikers in those days was to sing out as they smelled smoke, calling to any men in the woods with guns to let them know that you were just a hiker, not a government man. It wouldn't have been surprising to run into a still anywhere near Bent Mountain because the mountain was known as a moonshine producing area throughout Prohibition. That it was so wouldn't have surprised anyone in the 1930s, as making moonshine and apple brandy was an essential part of the fabric of life throughout the mountains of Virginia. In fact, given that the Bent Mountain plateau was, by the turn of the last century, a major apple producing area—tobacco having played out decades earlier—it is likely that many of those stills were producing apple brandy rather than classic moonshine from corn. By 1932, when Avery and the RATC rerouted the trail up and over Bent Mountain, Prohibition was still the law of the land, not that the end of Prohibition put a stop to the games of cat and mouse played by men making moonshine and the government agents trying to catch them. Franklin County, "the wettest county in the world," as some would have it, was just a few miles away to the east, and the thirsty markets of Roanoke and Salem were just north, so it's no surprise that making whiskey or brandy was an important part of the local economy.

When Avery came to Roanoke to help scout the trail, the region just south of the city was still recovering from one of the biggest snowfalls in local history. In early March, a blizzard of titanic proportions blew through, making even the one paved road from Roanoke to Floyd completely impassable, closing local schools for weeks and generally shutting down the entire region until the snow started to melt. Things were so bad that between the snow and the economic disaster of the Great Depression, the superintendent of the neighboring Floyd County Public Schools initially announced that he was closing the schools until the following fall and couldn't even guarantee that they would reopen in September, much to the disappointment of parents of local children. Although the schools eventually reopened, it was a snowstorm people remembered for decades.

Things had gotten bad for the Appalachian Trail south of Bent Mountain as well. Shirley Cole had left the area for work in Texas, leaving the trail unsupervised between Bent Mountain and Lovers Leap in Patrick County, more than thirty-five miles to the south. At Avery's urging, the Roanoke club took over supervision of Cole's section of the trail that year, an arrangement that continued until the trail moved west in 1952. As the minutes of the first annual meeting of the RATC point out, the trail between Bent Mountain and Patrick County was almost entirely on unused or disused roads, so maintaining the route mostly meant driving those roads from time to time to make sure the anodized aluminum trail markers with their distinctive Appalachian Trail logo were still visible on fence posts and road markers. Where the trail departed the road, RATC members had to visit with the farmers whose land the trail crossed when it jogged between one country lane and another—farmers like Doug Bell's grandfather outside Copper Hill in Floyd County.

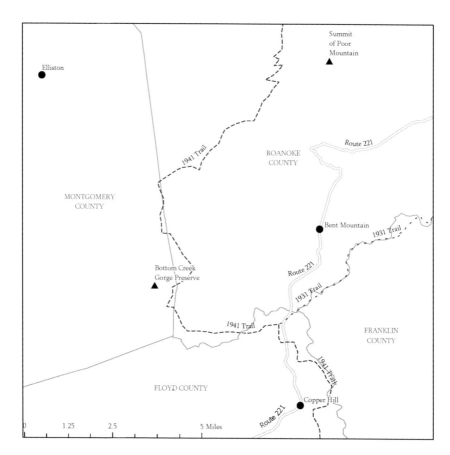

Appalachian Trail: Between Elliston and Copper Hill

▲ Landmarks	**N**	----- 1941 Trail		
● Towns		- - - 1931 Trail		
▢ Country Borders		══ Highways		

MAP 4 Appalachian Trail between Elliston and Copper Hill. *Map created by Timothy Sproule.*

FLOYD COUNTY

By coming to know a place where the common elements of life are understood differently one has the advantage of an altered perspective. With that shift, it is possible to imagine afresh the way to a lasting security of the soul and heart, and toward an accommodation in the flow of time we call history, ours and the world's.
—*Barry Lopez,* Artic Dreams, *1986*

Doug Bell is a man who belongs exactly where he is. And where he was on a warm afternoon in May 2019 was standing in front of the foundations of his grandfather's farmhouse near Copper Hill in Floyd County. That land has been in the family for a very long time, and you can see the pride of it in Doug's face as he talks about his grandfather and about the land itself. We had walked up to the old homeplace along a mushy dirt road that began at the bottom of the hill so he could show me where the Appalachian Trail came across the farm and past his grandfather's front door. On the way there from the dream house that Doug and his wife, Arlene, are building just down the road, we passed the old Graysville store and the site of the Shady Fork School. The school was closed by the time the Appalachian Trail came to Floyd County and so was suggested as a good place to camp, but the store was still open and the owner, Howard Grey, would let hikers camp out back and would sell them a hot meal. Someone lives in the old store these days, but the school burned a few years ago and what was left was hauled off by somebody. Now the former schoolyard is just home to some blue plastic barrels and a few dead appliances that someone dumped there when no one was watching.

Doug Bell at his grandfather's farm in 2019. *Author's collection.*

In the way of the old Appalachian Trail, long before it became a national park in 1968, the trail just went where it went. Sometimes that meant it went around a community baseball field, skirting the sheds where the equipment was stored; sometimes it just went down the side of a highway; sometimes it went through a town park; and sometimes it went right down Main Street. And at least once it went right past a farmer's front door. Which is why Doug was standing where he was that May afternoon.

Just above the Bell family farm, the trail came through a small grove of white pines and then passed over an open field belonging to the family who farmed the land next door to the Bells and along the boundary of a cemetery with headstones for Waltons, Craigheads and others who found their last resting place on the slopes of that hill. At the top of the hill, hikers could look down at the Bell family farm. Standing there on the hill, they would have seen a large two-story white house with a granary and a long chicken coop a few dozen yards up slope from the front door, as well as a big red barn off to the right down the slope. The granary and the chicken coop are still there, but the house burned a while ago and the barn collapsed more recently. These days, Doug and Arlene's chickens live in coops made from bits and pieces of that old barn, a tangible connection between the Bells' new home and Doug's family place just down the road. Just behind their new house is a small pond where they dammed up the creek, and in the summer, bears come down to bathe and just splash around just for fun. Doug and Arlene would have built their dream home on the old farm, but the new place is more practical, being on a main road maintained by the county. When you live in a place where it snows hard in the winter, county road maintenance matters.

In 1930, the trail route Shirley Cole and Roy Ozmer picked out didn't cross the Bell family lands. Instead, it followed the old Ridge Road on the other side of the hill. But then the Blue Ridge Parkway arrived in 1935, and the trail had to move. To get away from the highway construction, the RATC chose a new route that crossed over the Bells' farm and the one belonging to their neighbors up the slope to get hikers down to County Road 642, which then took them past the Graysville Store. It doesn't make any sense that the RATC folks would have taken the trail right between the coop and the granary and then up to the farmhouse door. But that's where it went. My guess is that Doug's grandfather may have changed to route a tiny bit just so that passersby would come closer to his house. "My grandfather used to tell stories about the hikers coming to the door and asking if they could buy eggs or other things to eat," Doug told me. Because he's only in his early sixties, Doug doesn't remember the hikers, of course. The last ones came through in 1952, before he was born. But he remembers the farm and the stories his grandfather told him about the men and women with their backpacks who stopped by on their way south or north.

There are plenty of places where the trail still passes close to someone's home, but I can't think of a single one where it goes right up to their front door. In these times of high anxiety about strangers, it's hard to imagine what it must have been like on the Bell farm. Hikers in those days didn't tend to be quite as scruffy as they are today, although as he passed by the farm in 1948, Earl Shaffer did comment in his diary that with his sunburn and long hair standing up in the wind, he must have been quite an unusual sight for anyone who saw him. Most, though, wore respectable

Bell family farm, circa 1920. *Used with permission of Doug Bell.*

hiker clothes and high lace-up boots, looking a bit like they jumped out of an L.L. Bean or Abercrombie & Fitch catalogue picture. And even Shaffer did his best to shave when he could so that people wouldn't think he was a hobo or, worse, a communist. Doug and I talked about this while we stood there in front of where his grandfather used to live. "I think one of the big problems in America today is that people just don't trust each other anymore. It used to be okay to walk across someone's land, but it's not anymore. And if you had a problem, people would come and help. It feels like we've lost that," he told me.

Everywhere I've been along the old route of the Appalachian Trail in Southwestern Virginia, people I've spoken with express a similar nostalgia for a time when you trusted your neighbors, when everyone knew everyone else and when people depended on one another. "I'm worried about my little town," Kim Turman told me when I met her back in October 2018. Kim works in the county agricultural extension office in Floyd, and I'd gone there to see if they had any records about Shirley Cole from his time as the county's first extension agent. "So much is changing. Our farmers are really stressed. We've even created a program for them called 'Weathering the Storm' to help them deal with all the things that are putting pressure on them. Tariffs, environmental changes, things like that. It's just not like it used to be." And that was almost two years before COVID-19 arrived in our lives. Of course, a lot of this nostalgia is for an imagined past, not the one people actually lived in, because things were hard in the 1930s when the trail first appeared. Very hard. It was, after all, the time of the Great Depression. At 101, Cole's daughter Dorothy Shifflet remembers that real past though. "People were coming to the door all the time wanting to spend the night or to ask for food. The bottom just fell out of everything. People didn't even have anything to eat." Great Depression or not, Cole and his friends, with the support of Avery, his PATC volunteers and later the RATC, brought the Appalachian Trail to and through Floyd County, leaving behind traces that you can still see if you know where to look.

The trail entered Floyd County just south of Bent Mountain and climbed the slopes of Smith Mountain (3,368 feet) between Adney Gap to the north and Sweet Anne Hollow to the south, ascending rapidly to the top of the mountain. From the summit, hikers could look north to Roanoke; northeast all the way to the Peaks of Otter, where Ozmer first started his route-finding expedition; east into Franklin County; southeast to Cahas Mountain (3,571 feet); or all the way south to mighty Buffalo Mountain (3,960 feet), just a little south of the town of Floyd. The trail didn't cross Buffalo Mountain, but hikers were encouraged to take a side trip to its summit, where, if you squinted just a little, you could see all the way to the Unakas on the west side of the New River. Smith Mountain wasn't quite that good, but according to Avery, the views from the summit of Smith Mountain were among the best along the entire trail in Southwestern Virginia. Those views were so good that in his notes on his first visit to that part of the trail, Avery dubbed them "spectacular" because they took in the entire eastern bend of the Blue Ridge Mountains south of Roanoke and down toward Fisher's Peak on the North Carolina border where the ridgeline bent west again.

From Smith Mountain, the trail descended onto the old Ridge Road along the edge of the Great Escarpment, leading hikers through one water gap after another. If they felt like the entire trail in Floyd County was just a long series of water gaps, they weren't far wrong, as it's a fact that there are more than two dozen different named streams running off the plateau to the west and down into Franklin County to the east. Every one of those streams had several millennia to carve a gap in the escarpment, and when the trail left the roadbed, hikers had to walk down and then back up again through those gaps. Some of the gaps dipped only a little, but others went down quite a bit, so much so that hikers might just have named this section of the trail

Smith Mountain from the Appalachian Trail in 1932. *Appalachian Trail Conservancy Archives.*

the Roller Coaster had it stuck around long enough to have been hiked by thousands rather than hundreds of hikers. Instead, that name stuck to the section just south of Harpers Ferry, where it briefly feels like you do nothing but hike up, then down, then up, then down again for most of a day.

Once the Blue Ridge Parkway construction began in 1935, the Ridge Road route was co-opted by the highway planners and so the ATC had to move the trail. The bad part was that all those water gaps really came into play. The good part, though, was that the trail shifted to some more interesting locations, like the Bell family farm and Pumpkin Stem Knob, where the views were described as even better than spectacular—they were "extraordinary" and "should not be missed." Those extraordinary views are gone now because the knob, once cleared land, has grown over entirely, and all you can see from the summit are the trunks of poplars and oaks. The few driveways that lead to the summit either have gates or "No Trespassing" signs.

All those views, though, spectacular or extraordinary, didn't amount to much if you were hungry. And backpackers do get hungry. When Ozmer and Cole laid out the original route of the Appalachian Trail south from the Peaks of Otter, there were no stores along the trail's route until you

Pumpkin Stem Knob in 2019. *Author's collection.*

got to Thompson's Store on Pumpkin Stem Knob. When the RATC and Avery rerouted the trail across Catawba Mountain a few years later, hikers could obtain supplies in several places like Mason Cove and Bradshaw, but once they started to climb Poor Mountain, they wouldn't pass another store without diverting off trail until they reached Thompson's. The Thompson Store still stands right where the hikers would have passed it in 1933 or 1952, but these days it appears that someone uses it for storage; unless someone cleans it up soon, the vines and briars that are climbing all over the building will completely encase it in a thick green shell and eventually will pull it down altogether.

By 1950, there was another option for hikers close by. The old Kelley School had been converted into a store. In fact, Arlene Bell worked there when she and Doug were first married more than forty years ago. Like the Thompson Store, the store in the old Kelley School building still stands, but unlike the Thompson Store, the Kelley School is just there, unlocked, its front door sprung open, for anyone to wander around in. The store closed decades ago and the floors are coated in a deep layer of dust, but

The Kelley School along the Blue Ridge Parkway in 2019. *Author's collection.*

you can still see the ghostly outline of the old counter. Behind it, the shelves are still labeled, but the ink on those labels is so faded that it's impossible to know what might have been on those shelves. It's not hard to imagine, though, because the stock in stores like the Thompson Store and the one at the Kelley School was pretty typical wherever you went—necessities like coffee, flour, matches, cigarettes, cornmeal, vinegar and salt; novelties like candy, honey, tea bags or candles; maybe some fancier spices like cinnamon, especially when it was time to make apple butter; and hardware like screws and nails, door hinges and panes of glass. There might have been cloth wrapped around bolts or a few books and magazines. Each storekeeper tried to stock what was needful in his or her community, and they knew everyone by name. People kept accounts that they settled up at the end of the month or when they got paid or sold their crops.

If you've ever lived in a small rural community, you know just how important the country store is to the life of the place. People come in for news or gossip; in many communities, the store and the post office share the same building, so they stop in for their mail and packages. They sit on the front porch and watch the world go by, hoping something interesting might happen, and the arrival of a backpacker or two certainly would have been something interesting in the 1930s. Imagine just for a moment what it must have been like when some of the first Appalachian Trail hikers came in through the front door of one of those little stores along the old trail route, hungry, thirsty and just a little ripe. A few of the men might have had beards, like Gene Espy when he walked by in 1951. Beards made people just a little bit nervous. But Espy was a southerner, albeit from Georgia, and had very nice manners, so any concern about his beard generally dissipated quickly. Chester Dziengielewski, on the other hand, would have made people sit up and stare. A machinist from Naugatuck, Connecticut, and the son of Polish immigrants, Dziengielewski was the third person (after Shaffer and then Espy) to thru hike the Appalachian Trail and the first to successfully hike it southbound. Like Espy, he passed by the Thompson Store in the fall of 1951. Dziengielewski kept himself shaved, but he was a sight, hiking in twill pants cut off at the knees with his pocketknife and carrying almost no gear at all. Instead of a tent, Dziengielewski had a sheet of plastic that he rolled up in if it rained. His cooking rig was a scorched old coffee can that he hung over the fire, and he used a nail to punch holes in cans of food he bought along the way. If he did venture into the Thompson Store that summer to buy some cans of food, what must the storekeeper and anyone else there have thought of him?

Whatever the storekeepers and their neighbors thought of the hikers who came in through the front door, those hikers confronted a very different assortment of dietary choices from those favored by backpackers today. There were no Pop-Tarts (invented in 1964) or packages of instant ramen (invented in 1958). There were no granola bars, which didn't hit the shelves until the 1970s. And there were no Slim Jims because although they had been invented in the 1940s, they didn't go into nationwide distribution until the mid-1950s, well after the trail had moved away.

So few hikers passed along the old route of the Appalachian Trail between 1930 and 1952 that it's unlikely that the small-town store keeper stocked up for "hiker season" between April and October, as countless do at stores along the trail today. That meant hikers had to make do with what they could find in the typical store. Accounts of hiking the Appalachian Trail in the 1930s and the 1940s turn out to be pretty consistent in their discussions of hiker food, some of which certainly could have been on offer at the little stores the hikers found between Roanoke and Damascus. For example, one set of recommendations for what to bring for two men on a ten-day hike on the Appalachian Trail in Maine in 1930 suggested a diet based on dried fruit (raisins, apricots), pancakes, bacon, dried soup, canned meat, rice, powdered milk, tea, baker's chocolate and onions. Another account of hiking the trail in Virginia in the 1940s suggested a diet rich in bacon and onion sandwiches, oatmeal, dried fruit, canned peaches, pancakes and rice, supplemented by whatever vegetables were available from farmers or stores along the way. Those early "grub lists" were also filled with canned meats (corned beef, chicken and, after World War II, Spam), and it's certainly conceivable that local stores stocked these items.

Dehydrated vegetables—onions, carrots, potatoes, corn, green beans and pumpkin—were all available by the early 1930s, but it's hard to imagine these little local stores stocking such things. Just as unlikely would be cans of College Inn Chicken à la King, which shows up often in advice articles for Appalachian Trail hikers, and Knorr Erbswurst, the key ingredient in "dynamite soup," almost certainly would have been unavailable. During my research, I kept finding references to this mysterious soup but couldn't locate a recipe or figure out the name. Finally, in early 2020, I found a letter in the archives of the East Tennessee Historical Society in which the author explains both the recipe and the name: "One of our mainstays is a soup or stew that is not always above suspicion. With a basis of a handful of rice we add any dehydrated vegetables in sight, especially onions, and a stick of *erbswurst*—also known, from its appearance and its later (explosive) qualities, as dynamite soup—with a little slab of chopped bacon and anything else that is lying loose around." Dynamite indeed.

Reading those old grub lists, a present-day hiker might wonder, as I did, how hikers managed carrying around a slab of bacon, especially on warm summer days. As it turns out, Abercrombie & Fitch, in those days the country's premier outdoor retailer, had solved that problem. Hikers who wished to carry along a nice slab of bacon needed only to purchase one of the company's "pork bags," which resisted grease and kept one's pack free of any messy fat that might want to leak all over their clothes or tent. One might also wonder what hikers did with all the empty cans their grub generated? In the early days of the Appalachian Trail, most shelters had a nearby trash pit where hikers were supposed to burn and bury their waste. In later years, the trash pits were (mostly) replaced by trash barrels, aka "bear magnets." Only since the 1970s have Appalachian Trail hikers been forced to hang their food from trees or place it in bear boxes. Given the lack of shelters along the old Appalachian Trail in Southwestern Virginia, hikers wouldn't have had access to either trash pits or barrels, so they did what hikers had done for generations—they burned their trash in their cooking fires and left the burnt cans behind for others to find.

Advertisement for College Inn's Chicken à la King in 1930. *Author's collection.*

The other long-distance hiker tradition that has largely, but not completely, ended was simply walking up to the door of a farmhouse, like Doug Bell's grandfather's, and asking the farmer if he or she would sell some eggs, meat, milk, vegetables or fruit. Accounts by hikers like Gene Espy and Earl Shaffer, but also others less well known because they didn't complete a thru hike and then write a book about it, mention that it was common for farm families to invite the hiker in for dinner. Emma "Grandma" Gatewood, the third woman to hike every step of the trail, was well known for knocking on doors to ask for food, and more than once she was invited in for meals. While hikers today still buy produce from local farms along the trail, and sometimes even are invited in for dinner, mostly that tradition has faded into the past.

Just south of the Thompson Store, the post–Blue Ridge Parkway version of the trail passed near the Smart View Park (now Recreation Area). Today, the Recreation Area—with its picnic tables, well-preserved settler cabin from the 1890s, excellent views and diverse bird watching opportunities—is a place for visitors to the parkway to stop, have a nice walk or eat a bite under the trees. They can also take a pleasant walk on a mountain trail, but those visitors must be excused for not knowing that at least part of their hike is on the old Appalachian Trail, as there are no signs and no interpretive information available to tell them that the trail once passed right through the park. In fact, at no point along the three hundred miles of the old Appalachian Trail route is there any sign or marker to indicate that American's most iconic long-distance hiking trail once passed that way.

County Line Baptist Church in 2019. *Author's collection.*

Just south of the Recreation Area, hikers came to the County Line Primitive Baptist Church, organized in 1869, which still stands today and where services are still held on Sundays during the warm months. Churches like the County Line church provided important landmarks for hikers along the Appalachian Trail in Southwestern Virginia for the simple reason that everyone knew where they were; if a hiker got lost, all he or she had to do was ask for directions to the church. These small churches also sat close to the very same roads the trail followed and so were easily spotted as hikers walked north or south. For example, the trail guide description of this particular section of trail reads, "Pass County Line Church on left; immediately after, at 25.02 turn sharp left on well-worn road." When we try to imagine life in Floyd, Patrick, Carroll or Grayson Counties in the 1930s, 1940s and 1950s, it's important to realize that people's lives were organized around the rhythms of the seasons—when to plant, when to pick, when to harvest, when to make apple butter, when to cut wood for the winter and when to can fruits and vegetables against the winter's needs. But they were also governed by the rhythms of family life, and family life was always organized, in large part, by church. Southwestern Virginia has a rich Protestant tradition, and that tradition is made manifest by the many tiny churches that dot the landscape. During one of my visits to Floyd, I was told that there are more Brethren churches in Floyd County than in any county in the United States. But there are also Methodists, Baptists, Primitive Baptists, Lutherans, Nazarenes and Presbyterians. In fact, it seems you can hardly drive (or hike) down a road in this region without passing a church after ten or fifteen minutes.

Today, Floyd is also home to another kind of organization for ordering people's lives. In addition to five or six dozen Protestant churches, Floyd County is also home to one of the largest concentrations of intentional communities in the United States. Driving through the back roads of the county today, it's not surprising to pass a quiet little brick or plank church with a neat cemetery out back or to the side and then, around the bend, come to a gate with Tibetan prayer flags snapping in the breeze that always seems to blow up in those hills. The intentional communities range from ashrams to communes, eco-villages, spiritual retreats and yoga centers. When I was in Floyd in 2019, I met the founder of one of those eco-communities. A fortyish woman with a nose ring and an armful of homemade bracelets made from brightly colored threads, she told me that she and her partner had bailed on life in the big city, in their case the Washington, D.C. area, and had come to Floyd County with their eight children to create an eco-community where, eventually, five families would live in proximity to one another, sharing a communal space for things like eating, games or telling stories. To me, it sounded a bit like commune-lite. Thus far, it hadn't been going especially well. They had managed to build only their own house and one for a second family, but because the second home didn't have electricity, no one had stuck it out for a full year. But they had hopes, dreams, a plan and determination. Listening to the almost messianic way she described that plan, I have to believe that they are going to make it work in the end. But wiring the other homes will definitely help. No such communities greeted Appalachian Trail hikers, though, because the migration of such folks to Floyd began in the 1960s, and by then the trail was long gone.

What those hikers of the 1930s, 1940s and early 1950s *would* have found was music, and not just any music. The music they would have heard coming from barnyards, music halls, church picnic pavilions and fairgrounds is known today as "old-time music." Old-time music, a term first applied to this genre by the marketing folks at Okeh Records in New York back in the early 1920s, is rooted in the plaintive ballads brought to Virginia by Scottish and Irish settlers and inflected by Protestant hymns, gospel music and other Black spirituals. But if you go to the Floyd Country Store on a Friday night, you'll see that this music is anything but sad and mournful. The Friday Night Jamboree began at the Country Store in the early 1980s and has become a fixture in the community, drawing musicians and tourists from all over the country and even from abroad. They don't come just to hear the music, though, because old-time music is not a style of music where you sit and listen. The music coevolved with dance, especially contra dancing, clogging and square dancing. As Dylan Locke, the current owner of the Country Store, told me, "This isn't entertainment. Old-time music is community. It's meant to have as many people take part as possible." I certainly saw that when I attended my first Friday Night Jamboree. As soon as the music began, couples, groups and individuals surged onto the dance floor and just danced with whomever was closest to them. As I watched, a young Virginia Tech coed twirled with a seventyish man in bib overalls, both of them smiling and laughing. Next to them, a middle-aged married couple tapped their feet and banged out a rhythm with their heels and a man in his thirties standing next to them clacked two spoons together on his hip. As Dylan put it, "The music and the dancing are connected. The musicians want the dancers to be happy. The dancers know they're there to give the musicians energy." Watching all that joy on the dance floor and up on stage, I had a brief vision of slightly scruffy hikers hopping, twirling and tapping their feet to this same music, welcomed into the crowd just as everyone is on Friday nights. The fact that there were no hikers there left me feeling just a little sad.

Even if they didn't want to come and dance at the Country Store on a Friday night, Appalachian Trail hikers certainly would have pointed their boots toward Floyd Fest, an annual music festival that for years has taken place right on the boundary between Floyd and Patrick Counties. The very first Floyd Fest in 2002 featured Doc Watson and the Neville Brothers as the headliners, and over the years, the festival has drawn an ever more diverse set of performers ranging from local musicians to well-known recording artists including Ani DiFranco, Los Lobos, the Drive-By Truckers, Buddy Guy, Lauryn Hill, Emmylou Harris and Gregg Allman. But Floyd Fest isn't just about the music. People camp out, take yoga classes, visit craft demonstrations, eat, drink, relax, make new friends and are just part of what is, really, a celebration of community and the arts. Of course, hikers would have targeted Floyd Fest—how could they not? For one thing, it would have been hard to miss. Although almost no one knows it now, the road attendees take to get to the festival site was, for many years, the route of the old Appalachian Trail. And when they got there, pitched their tents and settled in for several days and nights of music and fun, they would have been taking part in a tradition more than two hundred years old. "Life in the mountains revolved around working hard," Dylan Locke told me. "At the end of a hard workday, they would gather to dance, make music and maybe drink a little." If there is one thing that the old route of the Appalachian Trail would have contributed to the hiking experience, it would have been the opportunity to gather, dance, make music and maybe drink a little.

SOMETHING HIDDEN?
GO AND FIND IT

The past has a way of luring curious travelers off the beaten track.
—*Keith Basso,* Wisdom Sits in Places, *1996*

Pretty much any historian will tell you that archives are dangerous places. We go into an archive with a plan in mind, or at least some questions we hope to answer, and start asking archivists for maps of this, letters about that, documents, photographs, reports or whatever else we can think of and hope to find cool things. The danger arises when those cool things start showing up at the desk where we're working; sometimes we open a box and a rabbit hole appears right in front of us, beckoning us down into its dimly lit depths. Mostly we do our best to stay on the beaten track, to ignore those rabbit holes and the siren songs emanating from them. But sometimes the lure is just too great and we can't resist jumping in to see what's down there. That's exactly what happened to me almost three years ago when I was in the archives of the Appalachian Trail Conservancy in Ranson, West Virginia. I was researching the early days of the Appalachian Trail and had been looking for information about how the trail was scouted south of the Potomac River. In one of the boxes I opened, I found some letters between Myron Avery and Shirley Cole from 1930 and was confused. The trail didn't run through Floyd County. From Dragon's Tooth just south of Roanoke, it veered southwest toward Pearisburg. But those letters told a different story. And there it was: a rabbit hole. Did I want to stop what I was doing and learn more about an abandoned part of the trail, or did I want to stick with my research plan? Honestly, if I hadn't spent the first five years of my life in Franklin County, right next door to Floyd, I probably would have stuck to the original plan. But I *did* spend the first five years of my life in that part of the state, and so I jumped into the rabbit hole to see what was down there.

For several years, I have been posting information about my research to a website called Appalachian Trail Histories, and right around the time I jumped into that rabbit hole, I received an e-mail from a man named Jim McNeely, who lives outside Pearisburg. As it happened, I had encountered Jim, or at least his writing, a year earlier in a newspaper article questioning whether Earl Shaffer really was the first successful thru hiker. The author of that article quoted Jim extensively, and I later read part of the online report Jim had written summarizing his findings about Shaffer's hike. In that first e-mail, Jim wrote, "I suggest that remarkably if not uniquely as to the many Appalachian Trail sections abandoned over the course of development of the current AT, the history of the OAT [Old AT] in southern Virginia is still ongoing because the Old AT is still very much present in the landscape and the culture." Because I was already looking into the history of this section of the trail, Jim's e-mail somehow convinced me that jumping into that rabbit hole hadn't been such a bad idea after all, and so when he suggested that I make contact with Randall Wells at the Partnership for Floyd, it seemed like a good idea. Randall turned out to be very enthusiastic about my plans and invited me to a meeting put on by the Partnership at the local public library, which, to my surprise, attracted an audience of more than thirty-five people. Jim McNeely was right. People in the region were still very interested in the old AT. I was hooked.

Jim wasn't there that day, but on a subsequent visit to Floyd, he and I met at the Hardee's at the north end of town, where he told me more about his connection to the trail and its history. It turns out that Jim is a thru hiker himself, having hiked the entire trail in 1985. Like so many Appalachian Trail hikers, Jim's experiences on the trail were transformative. The happy, positive people he met on the trail impressed him with how much fun they were having and how easily they related to one another. He liked that. After his hike, Jim returned home, got a law degree and even ended up in the state legislature for a time. He's retired from politics now but still practices a little law here and there. Mostly, though, he spends as much of his free time as he can out on the trail with his old dog, Princess Geva, or in archives, these days mostly focusing on understanding all the various re-routings of the trail over the past century. In fact, the more I've gotten to know Jim McNeely, the

Left: Jim McNeeley and Princess Geva in 2019. *Photo by Jim McNeeley.*

Below: The Appalachian Trail in Floyd County, 2019. *Author's collection.*

more he reminds me of Roy Ozmer. I can well imagine Jim out in the woods, scouting a new route for the trail at the behest of the folks up in Washington, writing long, detailed and sometimes beautifully worded reports about the beauty of the forests and the mountains.

The day Jim took me on a drive to see the old routes of the trail, it was cold, dreary, foggy in places and spitting rain most of the time. We piled into his old Chevy Astro van. "They say you double the value of an Astro van when you fill it up," he told me, and it was in the van that I met Princess Geva, a big, gray, muzzled boxer mix who is about as sweet as dogs get. The back of that van was her lair—Jim had pulled the seats out so she'd have more room and so he could keep his hiking gear at the ready. For the next four hours, we covered much of the old route of the trail east of the New River, stopping only for lunch at Aunt Bea's BBQ in Galax. It was there that Jim explained more about his obsession with Shaffer's hike. "I'm lazy," he told me. "But once I start wondering about something, I want to know all of it. I don't care so much about the bigger picture. I just want the facts." The facts Jim has found about Earl Shaffer's 1948 hike have convinced him that Shaffer skipped a number of sections of the trail in Southwestern Virginia and in Shenandoah National Park, which would mean Gene Espy was the first true thru hiker. Not everyone agrees, of course, and the Appalachian Trail Conservancy still formally recognizes Earl Shaffer as the first thru hiker. But Jim is a persistent man and never passes up an opportunity to explain why Espy was first.

Jim McNeely really is the master of facts when it comes to the routes of the old trail in Southwestern Virginia. To you or me, the old gravel road pictured here just looks like an old gravel road. But Jim can tell you that this was the trail's route in southern Floyd County in 1931 or in 1940 or in 1952. Honestly, if it weren't for Jim, whose motto (taken from Horace Kephart) is "Something hidden; go and find it," I would have spent countless and likely fruitless hours trying to puzzle out the various routes of the trail. Instead, I had Jim, who knows it all. I'll admit that there were times during our driving tour of the old trail routes that I wished he would slow down a little or turn on his windshield wipers in the rain, but I lived to tell the tale and will always be grateful to Jim for spending the day sharing with me the world he's come to know so well.

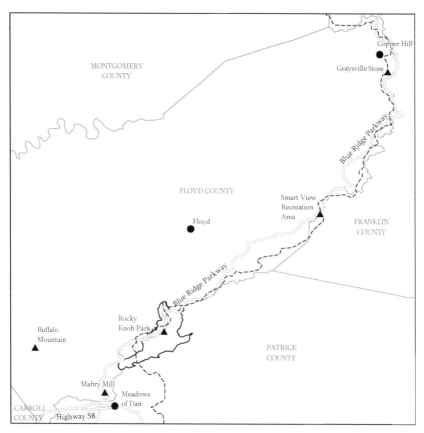

Appalachian Trail: Between Copper Hill and Meadows of Dan

Landmarks

Towns

Parks

N

Roads

1941 Trail

County Borders

Map 5 Appalachian Trail between Copper Hill and Meadows of Dan. *Map created by Timothy Sproule.*

PINNACLES OF DAN

We had a little paradise here. There used to be chestnuts. Everyone had pigs and you would just turn them loose. Notch their ears so everyone knew whose was whose. Then they would eat chestnuts and get really big. No one took anyone else's pig. Not like now, when people don't trust each other.
—Ralph Lee Barnard, 2019

Climb to the top of Rocky Knob, just off the Blue Ridge Parkway, and you'll find the only hiker shelter ever constructed along Virginia's Lost Appalachian Trail. A three-sided stone structure built by the Civilian Conservation Corps in 1937, the old shelter once provided an overnight stopping point for Appalachian Trail hikers headed north or south along the trail. Today, it's a place where people go for a quick and easy jaunt up from the Saddle parking lot in the Rocky Knob Recreation Area along the parkway. On a good day, you can see for thirty or forty miles east from the Saddle wayside. On a foggy day, you can barely see your hand in front of your face. On the good days, people often stop there for lunch or a snack. On the foggy days, they peer out into the gloom, maybe read the interpretive sign and keep going. Sometimes they hike up the hill just to the south of the parking area to the old trail shelter and take a few pictures there, but they'd be forgiven for not knowing they were on the original route of the Appalachian Trail or that legendary Appalachian Trail hikers stayed there once upon a time; like everywhere else along the original route of the trail, there is no sign or marker to tell them that this was once a link in America's oldest long-distance hiking trail. Earl Shaffer reported spending a cold and windy night there back in 1948. Today, it's just a place to walk to.

Rocky Knob Shelter along the old Appalachian Trail in 2019. *Author's collection.*

But if you do go and look out over the Piedmont down below, the views really can be quite spectacular, with row after row of low ridges defining the increasing amounts of open and very green space in between. Out to the east, just beyond those ridges, the mountains fail altogether and the rolling farmlands of Southcentral Virginia begin, and you can imagine, for just a minute, what it must have been like to reach that beautiful spot at the end of a long day of hiking, setting up your bedroll and cooking your dinner before falling into a well-deserved sleep. Go stand at the lookout just beyond the shelter today, and if you look straight down you'll be gazing into Rock Castle Gorge, one of the most beautiful spots in the entire region. The gorge was home to the Cherokee for centuries before white settlers arrived, and it was those later arrivals who named it "rock castle" after the quartz pinnacles along the wall of the Great Escarpment that reminded them of castle turrets. Follow the old Appalachian Trail south, and before long, you can turn east and down into the gorge, looping along Rock Castle Creek for several miles before climbing back up to the parking area below the old shelter. It's a challenging hike but well worth it.

If a steep downhill and then uphill hike isn't on your itinerary, from the shelter you can peer around to the south, and when the afternoon sun is just starting to slip down toward the edge of the ridge behind you, you might see a reflection off a smallish pond down below, just off Belcher Road. That pond holds the headwaters of the Dan River, once upon a time one of Virginia's most important waterways. From that little pond, the Dan flows south and east more than two hundred miles until it merges with the waters of the Roanoke River in Kerr Reservoir and vanishes. The Dan River is still the signature feature of the old mill town of Danville, but instead of providing power to the Dan River Mill, which shut down in 2006, the river is just a slightly toxic and mostly greenish-brown thing, horribly polluted by Duke Energy back in 2014 when one of its coal ash pits upstream in Eden, North Carolina, ruptured and dumped almost forty thousand tons of toxic sludge into the river, killing almost everything in sight. Swim at your own risk and do not eat the fish whatever you do. But up in Floyd and Patrick Counties, there is no hint of man's violence against nature. There the Dan River is still pristine and gorgeous.

From the shelter at Rocky Knob, you can't see any of the sadness and degradation of what was once a beautiful river. You can see the beginnings of the Dan River Gorge, though, way off to the right, and that is a place worth visiting. Possibly the most spectacular single piece of physical geography in the entire state of Virginia, the gorge has been described in glowing terms as "Virginia's Grand Canyon" and as one of "the signature features of this most spectacular region." The names of places around and in the gorge

The Little Falls of Dan in 1935. *Appalachian Trail Conservancy Archives.*

Townes Diversion Dam and Resorvoir from Rim of Dan River Gorge

Townes Diversion Dam, Patrick County, Virginia, in 1936. *Author's collection.*

invite even the most casual hiker to want to know more, to go down a trail and to scramble up and over a summit—Lovers Leap, the Indian Ladder, Devil's Footprint, the Pinnacles and more. When the Appalachian Trail was first laid out in this part of the state, there was a series of mighty cascades at the bottom of the gorge, waterfalls that people would spend all day hiking to, scrambling down steep and stony paths just to bathe their feet in the pools at the base of giant boulders or to fish for native brook trout in the deep pools beneath the falls. And then they'd hike back up, maybe over the Pinnacle itself, before finding their way back to their car and dinner at the little café in Meadows of Dan. It was quite a spot, once upon a time.

The canyon is still there, of course, because there is no coal in those mountains, so no one came to scrape the mountains away. The falls though? Some of them are underwater now, way down at the bottom of Talbott Lake, because in 1938, the City of Danville completed a hydroelectric project that included two dams in the gorge, filling up large portions of what was once a spectacular canyon that inspired travel writers to lyrical excess. Others are still there but see less water than they once did because so much is captured in the lakes above. When the dams were built to provide power to the mills in Danville, the Appalachian Trail had to move. Not far, but still away from those beautiful waterfalls. Hikers still had to climb up the harrowing Indian

Ladder if they were headed north or scramble down it if they were headed south. And either way, they had to traverse the Pinnacles, which was no easy feat. "It was really hard. Really difficult," Gene Espy told me in 2019, describing his hike over the Pinnacles in 1951. "Really difficult," he added, just to make sure I understood.

When Shirley Cole and Roy Ozmer made their scouting expeditions east of the New River, the Dan River Gorge called out to them both. Cole knew the area, of course, and was friendly with John Barnard, the man who had been taking hikers into the gorge for two decades. In fact, Barnard had a thriving side business in guiding hikers into the gorge on the weekends and during the summer when he wasn't teaching at one of the local schools. It was, therefore, an almost foregone conclusion that Cole and Ozmer would work with Barnard to figure out how to get their trail route from Floyd County down through the gorge that was quite literally in John Barnard's backyard.

Of all the characters who populate the story of Virginia's Lost Appalachian Trail, John Barnard is perhaps the most interesting and most complex. Born in Patrick County in 1885, Barnard lived his entire life on the family farm just south of Meadows of Dan, property that came to the Barnards as part of a three-thousand-acre land grant after the Revolutionary War. In 1930, when the Appalachian Trail headed his way, Barnard was a schoolteacher, a sometime member of the county board and a relentless promoter of economic development in the western (and mountainous) half of Patrick

John Barnard leading a hike on the Pinnacles of Dan in 1936. *Personal collection of Ralph Barnard.*

County. He advocated for and later helped survey the Blue Ridge Parkway and pushed hard for the building of the dams in the gorge behind his home because he was a firm believer in economic progress. Any project that was likely to bring jobs and tourists to the upper part of Patrick County seemed like a good idea to him. From his farm on what today is known as Squirrel Spur Road, Barnard regularly took groups of hikers down into the gorge to the waterfalls; led trout fishermen to some of his favorite pools along the Upper Dan; spent countless hours looking for, finding and collecting Native American artifacts; kept track of meteorological data for the state; and eventually helped Shirley Cole and Myron Avery carve a route for the Appalachian Trail through the gorge and over the Pinnacles. Most of that route, according to his grandson Ralph Lee Barnard, who I interviewed for the first time in 2019 and twice more since, was on trails that Barnard had already marked out and cleared for the hikers who came to his farm and paid him to guide them down into the gorge. Because the gorge was practically in Barnard's backyard—the Pinnacles were less than three miles from his front door—his tidy little farm was a perfect jumping-off spot for such hikes, especially once the Blue Ridge Parkway came within a quarter mile of his front door.

Before I met Ralph Barnard, several people told me that he had a reputation for being crusty and difficult. Ralph, like his grandfather, is anything but difficult and showed no signs of being crusty. On my first visit, he and his wife, Hope, welcomed me into their home, and he told me many wonderful stories about growing up at his grandfather's, with the Appalachian Trail more or less in the backyard. He also shared with me a number of the photos that appear in this book. On a subsequent visit, Ralph and I sat on the front porch during a brief rain shower, watching the barn swallows swoop across the front lawn, and talked about life in Meadows of Dan, about the trail and about the world in general. Now in his eighties, Ralph laughs at the least little thing, and like so many people I've met in Southwestern Virginia, he is sad about the many ways we seem to be losing our sense of community, our connection to neighbors and our love of the land. Once the rains stopped, Ralph took me on a driving tour of the rim of the Dan River Gorge, showed me the Townes Dam from above and took me to two different vantage points for seeing the Pinnacles, one of which we reached by just turning off the road and crossing the stubble of a neighbor's hay field in Ralph's new SUV. He introduced me to the head of maintenance for the Primland Resort, who took me on an ultimately fruitless hunt for the so-called Devil's Footprint—a rock that has what appears to be the impression of a demon footprint in it and is mentioned in a number of the trail guides from the 1930s. Then we dropped down the mountain to the Kibler Valley below the dams, and Ralph told me the story of his family's arrival in the valley, how they had prospered there and how, in the end, almost everyone had left. It could have been the story of almost any rural place in America today. People come, make a new life for themselves and their industry brings initial prosperity, but that success eventually fails, the small towns and the farms begin to decline, people start moving away and, before long, there are just memories held by a few of the old people who stayed behind. People like Ralph.

In 1949, *National Geographic* writer Robert Brown journeyed along the length of the Appalachian Trail with photographer Robert Sisson and subsequently wrote the first story about the trail to reach a truly national audience. One of the thousands of readers who were inspired by Brown's article was a farm wife in Ohio named Emma Gatewood. Writing about the route of the trail through Southwestern Virginia, Brown told of meeting John Barnard, the "King of the Pinnacles." When Brown arrived unannounced at Barnard's home, the same house where Ralph Barnard lives today, he knocked on the front door and was greeted by "a tall man with gentle eyes" who said that, yes, Brown could stay the night. Barnard told his guest to sit a bit on the front porch because he still had chores to do. "I tipped gently back and forth in a rocker. Black clouds banked up. It was quiet as a desert night. The shower broke and drenched the well-trimmed lawn, the round bed of geraniums ringed with pansies, and the rose bushes along the fence. A spate of water gurgled down the drainpipe." Reading Brown's account several months after I sat on that same porch during a summer storm, I was struck by how little had changed at the Barnard farm.

Before long, Barnard returned from his chores, and Mrs. Barnard invited the two men inside to eat. "Bowls of vegetables and stewed fruit, platters of meat, plates piled high with hot biscuits and cornbread, pitchers of milk and cream, jars of honey and homemade jam crowded the table. There were squash, string beans, and mashed potatoes; hot veal and cold ham; applesauce and pears; and quantities of sweet farm fresh butter to slather on the hot breads. What a feast!" he wrote of that evening meal. After dinner, Brown stayed in the Barnard family guest room and fell asleep to the rumbles of a distant thunderstorm. The next day, Barnard took his guest over the Pinnacles, a hike that he described as going up, around and over "huge broken rock masses intertwined with trees and shrubs," leading to the summit that crowned a peak with drops more than one thousand feet to the river below. With hospitality like that, it's no wonder

ATC chairman Myron Avery gave Barnard responsibility for the trail in Patrick County and visited him often.

Avery's decision to hand over control of the trail south of Floyd County came shortly after the completion of the route through Southwestern Virginia because already in 1932 Shirley Cole had vanished from the story of the Appalachian Trail. Unlike Cole, Barnard was rooted in the region and was a dependable correspondent. Avery also promoted Barnard's home as a place where hikers could secure "very comfortable accommodations and excellent food," as Robert Brown learned fifteen years later. In addition to providing a nice place to stay and eat dinner, Barnard was just the kind of man Avery liked: an experienced woodsman, self-reliant, interesting to talk to and willing to take direction from Avery. Avery was frankly worried about the fate of the trail in what he called "this most spectacular region" because it was so far from Washington and because there was no strong local organization to support the upkeep of the trail route. North and south of the gorge weren't going to be real problems because on the east side of the New River the trail's route was almost entirely on old or abandoned roadbeds and so didn't require much upkeep. But in the gorge was another story altogether, as keeping the trail open there was going to require "considerable clearing of underbrush" and constant attention to trail markings lest hikers become lost in what was a potentially dangerous place. After hiking from Lovers Leap (on the north rim of the gorge) to the New River in March 1933, Avery arranged to have this section of the trail kept in good shape by having the Virginia trail clubs in Roanoke, Lynchburg and Washington, D.C., send crews down once a year and, in between, paying Barnard an annual fee of ten dollars for keeping the trail marked and bushwhacked, an arrangement that stayed in place until the trail left the gorge in 1952. Although ten dollars a year doesn't sound like much today, it helps to understand that in those days, the ATC was very poor and regularly had to beg its member trail clubs for donations. A typical donation from one of those clubs in the 1930s and 1940s was ten dollars. So, in the context of the ATC budget, ten dollars a year was handsome pay, even if it didn't mean all that much to Barnard, who earned many times that amount each year trapping mink along the banks of the Dan. Avery also made regular use of Barnard's farm as a jumping-off point both for hikers and for trail workers, and everyone who stayed at the farm paid the Barnards for their board. Ralph remembered that when he was a teenager, one of his main jobs was to remind those hikers that smoking was forbidden in the barn. The Barnards depended on that barn and couldn't risk having careless hikers burn it down.

Potomac Appalachian Trail Club hikers at the Barnard farm in 1933. *Personal collection of Ralph Barnard.*

Hiking in the gorge was very different during the two decades that the Lost Trail passed through Patrick County. For one thing, the building of the Dan River Power Company dams had "messed things up considerably" down along the river, as Myron Avery put it in a letter to a friend in 1936. But even with that construction and flooding, it was still possible to hike through the gorge as long as one had the fortitude and wasn't too risk averse. "I remember the hikers," Ralph Barnard told me in a recent interview. "They would sometimes stay in the barn or just camp here in the yard out back. Some of them had the awfulest tales. There used to be panthers and such here and they always talked about the panthers. They had a lot of panther stories. You know, a panther screams like a woman. Sometimes the hikers thought it was a woman they'd heard and were worried about it." There are no panthers down in the Dan River Gorge today because the last eastern mountain lions had all disappeared from Virginia by the 1950s. But lately, it seems that they might be returning based on an increasing number of sightings along the Virginia/West Virginia border, some of them now confirmed by state fish and game officials. Maybe Ralph Barnard will hear the scream of the panther from his back porch again; if there was ever a place that a mountain lion would like in Virginia, it's the Dan River Gorge.

The two trickiest parts of that original route through Patrick County that Barnard helped the trail scouts plot out were the scramble over the Pinnacles and the "Indian Ladder." The Pinnacles of Dan, described by Avery as

The Pinnacles of Dan in 1932. *Personal collection of Ralph Barnard.*

"undoubtedly one of the most remarkable areas of the entire A.T. system," is a singular pyramid-shaped mountain that appears to have been dropped directly into the middle of the gorge. Rising 1,000 feet from the river to its summit of just over 2,600 feet, the peak presents hikers with one of the most difficult and challenging hikes available in Virginia. And hikers do still traverse the summit from time to time. For example, a recent hiker wrote in an online forum, "The hike along the ridge to the pinnacle was exciting and probably the most dangerous hike I have ever done. You have to use your feet, knees, hands, and butt to scramble." The level of difficulty this hiker described isn't new. In his book *Walking with Spring*, Earl Shaffer describes the climb and descent in much the same terms. "It was rock work pure and simple, with a precipice on either side….On the far side it was necessary to go backward most of the time, along narrow ledges and clutching bushes to keep from falling." Why would the trail's planners send hikers up and down such a harrowing route? Shaffer recounts a story told to him by one of those trail planners. According to this story, Myron Avery and a crew of PATC trail builders from Washington were staying with Barnard to complete the marking of the Appalachian Trail in the gorge. While Avery was off to the south of the Pinnacles, the rest of the group decided to play a joke on him by taking the trail up and over the most difficult part of the summit, surely using the route Barnard had been taking hikers on for years. The crew expected Avery to reject this route as too difficult and dangerous, but being

Myron Avery, the PATC president and ATC chairman pronounced it a good choice. So, hikers had to go up and over the summit the hard way. Because Barnard had been leading hikers over the summit for more than a decade before Avery and his trail crew showed up, Shaffer's version of events doesn't quite add up, but it survives largely because choosing the most difficult route is the kind of thing Avery *would* have done.

The Pinnacles, which Avery called "most spectacular," also spawned at least one crazy story during the 1930s. The November 1933 edition of the newsletter of the Natural Bridge Appalachian Trail Club (Lynchburg) reprinted shocking news of the Pinnacles first reported in the Reidsville, North Carolina *Review*:

> *What must have been an appalling sight, if anybody was looking, happened over in Patrick County, near Stuart, the other day when the top of the mountain known as the "Pinnacles of Dan" suddenly slid off 1,200 feet into the Dan River. Nature lovers and mountain climbers of this and other countries will be sorry to learn of the tragedy which befell this beautiful and picturesque mountain peak. Reports from that locality are that the whole top of the main, or middle point of the Pinnacles has fallen off and plunged down the perpendicular northeast side of the mountain, 1,200 feet into the Dan River.*

Needless to say, the top of the mountain did not fall off as reported, and the origin of that particular story was never determined. I can well imagine the glee of whoever concocted such a yarn when they found out that some credulous newspaper reporter actually bought their hoax.

Even more harrowing than crossing the Pinnacles, especially if it had been raining (and it rains a lot in this part of Virginia), was the "Indian Ladder." Intrepid northbound Appalachian Trail hikers, having made it up and over the Pinnacles, had to ford the Dan and then climb what Shaffer described as "a sheer cliff grown solidly with rhododendron." The guidebooks published by the ATC blandly describe the ladder as "a traditional Indian trail." Those books were written north to south and so advise hikers to descend that traditional trail using "*extreme care*. Do not attempt to cross canyon unless there is a full three and a half hours of daylight." Even Ralph Barnard, who is very proud of his exploits as a young man hiking with his grandfather, described the Ladder as "not easy." The Ladder is still there today, of course, because it was chiseled into the side of the slope by the Cherokee a very long time ago, but you can't climb it any longer because a few years ago a guest at the nearby Primland Resort slipped, fell and died there. It is still possible to hike the Pinnacles, however, but first you need permission from the power company that operates the dams just to get into the area. And if you want luxury before and after your hike, you can stay at Primland for upward of $400 per night and can get a seaweed wrap or have a steam to work the kinks out after your adventure. What John Barnard would have thought of a resort hotel just on the other side of the gorge where he grew up is anybody's guess. Mine is that he would have been happy, as promoting economic growth in the uplands of western Patrick County was one of the main goals of his life, and for all their mindfulness retreats, yoga classes and espresso mud scrubs, Primland represents real money, some of which filters down to the local folks who work there.

Back in the 1930s, though, hikers had to choose less ritzy accommodations. Because there were essentially no trail shelters, nor any plan to build such shelters anytime soon, the ATC guidebooks for this section of the trail specify instead businesses and individuals who might offer hikers a bed to sleep in or a yard where they could put up a tent. At Lovers Leap, the *Guide to the Paths of the Blue Ridge* advised, "Here is located the Lovers' Leap Tavern and filling station with accommodations for six in three small cabins; meals obtainable." The tavern has been closed for a long time and most recently housed a birdhouse shop. But imagine for just a minute that the Appalachian Trail still passed by Lovers Leap and that thousands upon thousands of hikers— some trying to hike the whole trail, others just out for a week, a weekend or a day—passed by that tavern. Think of the number of cheeseburgers, baskets of French fries, bowls of ice cream and, of course, beers the tavern owners would be selling during the peak hiking season. In 2022, the number of thru hikers who would have passed nearby headed north or south was more than four thousand. That's four thousand additional meals, likely more than four thousand beers and some substantial number of cabin rentals, especially if those cabins had hot showers. Given that the largest number of thru hikers still head north, the Lovers Leap Tavern would be catching them right after they had traversed the Pinnacle and climbed the Indian Ladder. What are the odds they wouldn't target the tavern for an overnight stop? Day after day in would come sweaty, smelly, hungry and thirsty hikers arriving like a migration of some alien species, desperate to recharge their phones, silly grins on their faces when they see the sign that says "Beer. On. Off." Who knows, given the penchant of the hiker community to create traditions where none existed—think the Half Gallon Challenge, just to name one of the more famous traditions of the trail—the difficulties of the Dan River

Gorge just might have inspired those hikers to create something equally fun for the Lovers Leap Tavern stop.

After all, the story of Lovers Leap is one that surely would have appealed to the hiker imagination and has the advantage of almost surely being made up and thus all but impossible to test for its veracity. According to the official Virginia tourism website, the lovers who leaped from the ridge to their deaths in true Shakespearean form were the son of white settlers who were in the process of pushing the Cherokee out of the nearby mountains and Morning Flower, the daughter of the local chief. Like Romeo and Juliet, the two lovers hid their romance from their families but, of course, were eventually found out, threatened with dire consequences and shunned by their families and friends. Rather than be torn apart by the conflict between their peoples, the unnamed settler boy and his Native American girlfriend are said to have walked to the rim of the escarpment, where they threw themselves off, "ensuring they would be together forever." Like most such stories, this one is almost certainly untrue and is remarkably similar to more than a dozen similar "lovers leap" stories around the country. But with the power of the Internet and the Virginia tourism machine, this particular story will stick to that beautiful viewpoint for a very long time. True or not, though, Lovers Leap has a county park and a nice picnic area for those who want to see the amazing view to the north and west. I've been three times and have yet to see the view for the simple reason that each time the ridge has been fogged in. But pictures like the one here, by Myron Avery in 1932, give you a pretty good idea why he agreed to route the trail this way.

Given the appealing story of star-crossed lovers, their romance doomed by the conflict between their parents, one can only imagine what tradition Appalachian Trail hikers might create while sitting around their campfire behind the Lovers Leap Tavern. There is no such tradition, of course, because Myron Avery and the ATC yanked the trail west in 1952. Instead, there are just birdhouses for sale.

The view from Lover's Leap in 1932. *Appalachian Trail Conservancy Archives.*

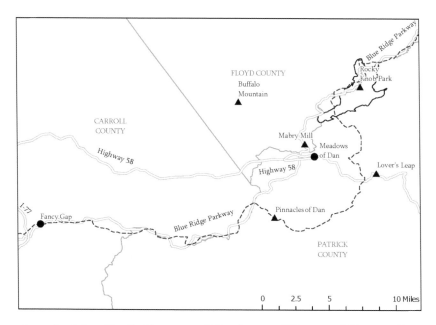

Appalachian Trail: Between Meadows of Dan and Fancy Gap

MAP 6 Appalachian Trail between Meadows of Dan and Fancy Gap. *Map created by Timothy Sproule.*

FOGGY CAMP

Walking creates trails. Trails, in turn, shape landscapes.
And, over time, landscapes come to serve as archives of communal knowledge
and symbolic meaning.
—*Robert Moor,* On Trails, *2016*

Have you ever really thought about fog? I mean really thought about it? Why it's so thick at one moment, like a mostly solid, immobile thing that makes you want to swim your arms in front of you just to move forward? Or why at other times it's like blowing wisps of gossamer, swirling, spreading, revealing details ahead of you and then randomly blocking them out again?

I'm sure scientists, at least some scientists, could explain why, in the space of five minutes, you can experience every kind of fog there is, which, as it turns out, is ten different kinds, ranging from good old-fashioned ground fog to hail fog, which I definitely do *not* want to experience. A scientist who actually understands fog could explain that fog begins to form when the difference between the air temperature and the dew point is less than 4.5 degrees. And of course, pretty much everyone has heard of the dew point, given how much the weathercasters on television or the radio mention it. If, however, you are like me and your eyes glaze over when the weather people get worked up over today's dew points, here's what it is: the dew point is whatever temperature air has to cool to before it becomes saturated with water vapor, at which point dew forms on surfaces like roads, grass, trees and most often your windshield. Don't ask why the dew point is different every

The Old Appalachian Trail at Fancy Gap in 2018. *Author's collection.*

day everywhere. There's a lot of math involved, so we'll just leave it at the fact that dew points can be, and almost always are, different. Which is why, I'm sure, it's so hard to predict when you're going to get socked in, up on a mountain, on a thin road or trail, in fog so thick you can't see a thing.

Now that we've established how fog happens, imagine the thickest fog you've ever been in—"upslope fog" caused by adiabatic cooling (again, don't ask)—and now imagine that the fog was even thicker than that. So thick that you can't see more than ten feet ahead of you. So thick that when you're driving on a two-lane parkway, you can't see the shoulder on the far side of the road. So thick that the two thin strips of yellow on your left and another thin strip of white on your right are the only things keeping your car from wandering off into the immense rhododendron bushes looming up on either side of the road like the walls of a medieval fortress. Or into the occasional massive oak, its limbs spread out and over you, casting dark shadows that just deepen the gloom. From time to time, single headlights appear suddenly, leather-clad riders nursing their motorcycles forward in the mists, passing just as slowly as you move in your car. The sound from their tailpipes is so muffled in the wet that you barely hear it. And then you're alone again in your bubble of gray, silent nothingness.

Welcome to what used to be the route of the Appalachian Trail in Carroll County. The elevation isn't that high in Volunteer Gap—not even 2,700 feet. But it's still a mountain. If the Blue Ridge Parkway was on one of *those* mountain roads, the kind with a sheer drop on one side or the other, driving through Volunteer Gap in the fog would be terrifying. Instead, it's oddly dissociative. There are no sheer drop-offs. No guardrails. No cliffs. No sense, really, that you are even up on a mountain, even though you are. Instead, there are just ancient rhododendrons, oaks and the occasional glimpse of a building, a field or a gravel road leading off into the mist. If it weren't for the motorcycles drifting in and then out of view, you'd feel like you were in one of those falling dreams—the kind where you just keep dropping through featureless grayness, where you can't get a single landmark and feel a rising sense of panic. In fog like that, the only choice you have is to keep going, so you just keep gliding forward. Fancy Gap is up ahead somewhere, and that's where you need to be. After even five minutes trying to drive through the fogs of the Great Escarpment of Southwestern Virginia, it won't come as a surprise to learn that the Cherokee supposedly preferred the name "Foggy Camp" for the area around Fancy Gap, or that white men kept the name for a very long time after they showed up and chased the Cherokee west. Fancy Gap is a very foggy place.

In fog this thick, it's easy to miss road signs because you can't see a thing. But just south of Volunteer Gap, there is an actual road with a real exit sign for an honest-to-God highway. Highway 52 isn't much as far as highways go, but in all that fog, it's a chance to loosen your grip on the steering wheel and maybe find some breakfast, which is how I found myself in the Lake View Motel Restaurant on a Saturday morning, sitting at the counter, feeling happy to be safely out of my car and waiting for some eggs, bacon, biscuits and grits. Today, it's not clear why in 1955 C.D. Phillips decided to call this restaurant the Lake View Motel because if you stand outside and look around, you won't see anything that looks like a lake. The motel across the highway is called the Mountain Top, which makes more sense. But if you look carefully next to the Lake View, on the other side of Devo Street, you can see where the "lake" used to be and where the motel was, laid out just on the other side. Now there is just a depression in the ground where the lake, really a pond, used to be, and the motel has long since been scraped off. In 1955, though, there was a lot more going on there at the intersection of Highway 52 and the Blue Ridge Parkway, most of it owned by C.D. Phillips and his son and most of it brand new, ready for the influx of tourists the parkway was bringing to the mountain. In addition to the Lake View

The Lake View Motel in 2018. *Author's collection.*

Motel and its restaurant, the Mountain Top Motel also had a restaurant, and just up the road, at least for a little while, was the Blue Ridge Court and its restaurant. These days, just the Mountain Top Motel and the Lake View restaurant remain, most of the business sucked away when Interstate 77 opened nearby back in the 1960s.

By the time I'd finished breakfast, the fog had lifted enough that I could see across the highway, so I strolled over to Antiques and Other Fanciful Things, owned by a man named Carl. It turns out that Carl loves history. Really loves it. But despite his love of history, he had no idea that once upon a time the Appalachian Trail passed right through the gap and that if it were still there, hikers would surely be congregating outside the Lake View after a breakfast like the one I just had. No Appalachian Trail hiker worth his or her salt passes up a breakfast like that when it's less than a quarter mile from the trail.

The 1934 edition of the *Guide to the Paths of the Blue Ridge* notes, "This section commences at the intersection (0 m.) of the 'Ridge Road' and U.S. Route 121 in Fancy Gap. Store and post office here; accommodations available at house of Mrs. Erna Webb, 1.9 miles north on U.S. Route 121."

Erna's gone now, of course. She died way back on March 12, 1943, and was buried at the Webb-Skyview Cemetery right there in Fancy Gap. "To a memory that gives us inspiration" is what it says on her headstone. But that house where she took in hikers and others just passing through Fancy Gap is all kinds of connected to the biggest thing to ever happen in Fancy Gap, or even in Carroll County, at least according to Carl.

"Gentlemen, I just ain't goin." That's what Floyd Allen said on March 14, 1912, when the judge in the courthouse up the road in Hillsville, the county seat, sentenced him to a year in prison for springing his nephews from the local jail, beating up the deputies who were guarding them and breaking the deputies' guns on a rock out front.

Having pronounced his unwillingness to spend a year behind bars, Allen started fumbling with this vest, apparently going for his gun, and all hell broke loose in the courthouse. To this day, folks in Carroll County debate who fired first, but more than enough shots were fired, fifty-seven in all. When the shooting stopped, five people were dead, including Judge Massie, who had refused to disarm everyone in court (a poor decision, as it turned out); Sheriff Webb; the commonwealth's attorney, William Foster; a juror; and a witness. Floyd was among the wounded and didn't get far, arrested nearby just a day later where he was laid up with a bullet in his pelvis. Floyd's brother Sidna managed to get all the way to Des Moines, Iowa, before hired detectives tracked him down six months later. It was Sidna who had built that big fine house in Fancy Gap where Erna Webb took in Appalachian Trail hikers.

The Sidna Allen House in 2019. *Author's collection.*

Because of the shootout, though, Sidna only managed to live there just a little more than a year. After what pretty much everyone now calls the "Courthouse Tragedy," the house was seized by the state and eventually sold to Sidna's lawyers, who then then sold it to Lewis Cassell Webb and his wife, Erna, who started taking in boarders as soon as they moved in. It was, and still is, a big house, maybe the biggest in Fancy Gap at the time, and it was too big for a married couple with just one child. Almost certainly that's why they took in boarders and then later hikers when the Appalachian Trail passed through town. By the time the Appalachian Trail arrived, Erna had outlived both Lewis and their son, Ewell, the only child they had, and she was still taking in boarders. Among those transients were surely some hikers on the new Appalachian Trail, since the guidebooks gave her house as the only place to rent a room for the night at Fancy Gap. Odds are she told those hikers all about Sidna, Floyd and the day all hell broke loose in the courthouse up in Hillsville. How could she not? But if she did, none of the few stories we have of those early hikes mentions it.

These days, there's a much easier way to get to Fancy Gap than the stately and foggy twists and turns of the Blue Ridge Parkway. Interstate 77 sweeps by just outside of town, and you can even stay at a newish EconoLodge for around fifty dollars and eat at the Kangaroo Express truck stop. But why would you? Back when the Appalachian Trail first came through town, it

The road to Fancy Gap in 1932. *Appalachian Trail Conservancy Archives.*

Fishers Peak   Sugarloaf

The Appalachian Trail from Fancy Gap in 1932. *Appalachian Trail Conservancy Archives.*

was a lot harder to get there. Until the federal government came along and built the Blue Ridge Parkway, Foggy Camp was a tough place to get to. If your plan was to get from the rolling Piedmont of North Carolina up onto the Great Escarpment or from the mountain down to the markets in Mount Airy, the gap that eventually became Fancy was one of the few logical routes to take up into or out of those mountains. The road that got laid down along Yankee Branch—named for the massacre of some Union soldiers camped at the headwaters of the creek by a few local men after the Civil War was already over—was popular enough that ever since the 1850s there has been some sort of inn or hotel in the gap. Eventually, that wagon road was extended all the way up into the Great Valley of Virginia, and travelers could ride to points north in coaches that bumped mercilessly on the mountain roads. To give you an idea of what the ride was like, just getting up the gap took those horse-drawn coaches five hours. When cars and trucks replaced the coaches, they had to stop about halfway up just to let their engines cool off from the climb. But by 1928, that old road—first an Indian path, then a white man's trail, then a wagon road and then a muddy track for cars—was finally paved, and people could actually drive up to Fancy Gap without stopping to cool off, without getting stuck and without having all their teeth bounced out. That old highway was eventually superseded by I-77.

Two years after the road was paved, Shirley Cole showed up in Fancy Gap with Roy Ozmer. If they chatted with anyone while they were there, and surely they did because Cole was a friendly man and a local boy, they would have announced that they were scouting out the route for a long-distance hiking trail from Maine to Georgia. What folks in the gap must have made of that idea no one now remembers. I'm sure, though, that they, just like the guests at the Hotel Mons, must have thought it was one of the craziest ideas they'd ever heard. Walk all the way to Maine? To Georgia? Why? Or maybe they thought it was the good kind of crazy, the same way that Ozmer had thought the first time he heard about the Appalachian Trail. Whatever the folks in Fancy Gap thought of the idea, Shirley Cole's plan that the Appalachian Trail would wind its way through his part of Southwestern Virginia caught on.

From the gap, the trail they laid out picked up the ridgeline again and headed southwest toward the North Carolina border. Cole and Ozmer decided that the route should cross over into North Carolina at Fisher's Peak (just south of today's Blue Ridge Music Center on the Parkway), both because the peak had excellent views down toward Mount Airy and because there was a place to stop called Norvale Crags, a popular picnic spot for folks driving up from "down the mountain" in North Carolina or over from nearby Galax. Fisher's Peak was also famous for its rhododendron thickets, described by hikers at the time as some of the most impressive they had ever seen. Southbound hikers thus crossed very briefly into North Carolina before turning back north and west toward the New River. Getting to the river meant getting across, and so Cole and Ozmer had to decide what to do about Galax.

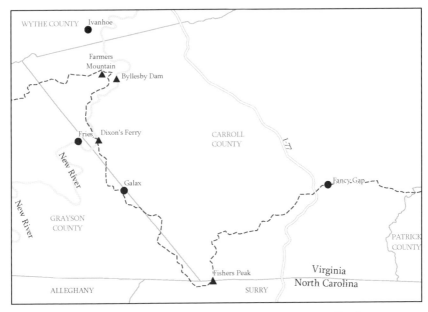

Appalachian Trail: Between Fancy Gap and Byllesby Dam

▲ Landmarks

● Towns

▢ County Borders

N

Rivers

– – – – 1941 Trail

Roads

Map 7 Appalachian Trail between Fancy Gap and Byllesby Dam. *Map created by Timothy Sproule.*

FURNITURE TOWN

*An enthusiastic meeting was held Tuesday evening in the ladies' parlor of
the Bluemont hotel at which the organization of a local Appalachian Trail
club was effected. R.E. Cox was elected temporary chairman and he and
Dr. Caldwell explained the purpose of the meeting and announced that the
Appalachian Trail Association was planning a Rhododendron Day celebration
and Festival to be held near Galax. Mr. Cox, who is a director of the
association, suggested that the most suitable place for the celebration would
probably be either Horse Knob or Fisher's Peak.*
—Galax Gazette, *May 31, 1931*

For all the ways that Shirley Cole frustrated Myron Avery, at first anyway,
Cole proved himself to be an excellent organizer. Even before he
received the ATC's mandate to start laying out the trail in his part of
the state, Cole began organizing Appalachian Trail clubs in the various
small towns east of the New River. The largest of those towns was Galax,
a furniture manufacturing center, and it was there that the largest of the
local AT-maintaining clubs formed. It was this club, led by R.E. Cox,
that decided to cut a road up to the summit of Fisher's Peak so they could
hold a Rhododendron Festival there, and it only made sense for the trail
to follow this new road. Shirley Cole's daughter Dorothy told me that the
Rhododendron Festival was all her father's idea, although local records don't
seem to bear that out. Regardless of whose idea it was, Fisher's Peak was
a perfect choice because it was both a scenic mountain covered in massive
rhododendrons and because it was only twelve miles from downtown Galax.

The road they cut way back in 1931 is still there and still called Fisher's Peak Road. In fact, there were so many large rhododendrons on the peak that the 1934 guide to the trail describes the road to the summit and the trail along it as "walled" by the bushes and says the summit had "rewarding views." Just south of those walls of beautiful flowering bushes, hikers on their way to Galax would have passed the "extensive recreational development" Norvale Crags, a popular destination for day trippers or weekend visitors from all over this part of Virginia and North Carolina. A local North Carolina newspaper described the Crags as being "one of the most beautiful knobs of the Blue Ridge," and it was also the spot where, in June 1931, Avery and Cole held an event dedicating the newly completed Appalachian Trail route from Roanoke to the New River. As evidence of Avery's ability to draw a crowd, attendees included a former governor of Virginia and the sitting governor of North Carolina. These kinds of events were very important for Myron Avery because one of his biggest concerns was that the trail clubs would finish building the Appalachian Trail and then no one would actually use it. The more publicity he could get for the trail, the better. From a hiker's perspective, though, the important thing about the Crags was that the clubhouse had a café that was well known for the excellent ice cream it served.

Once they left the Crags and headed back northwest toward Galax, hikers entered into one of those sections of the Appalachian Trail that the trail's planners would have liked to avoid but couldn't—an extensive stretch of road walking to get from one ridgeline to another. There were worse valley crossings on the trail—today's Carlisle Valley crossing in Pennsylvania comes to mind—but there weren't any others that took hikers right through the middle of an industrial town. But in 1930, Myron Avery and his team faced a choice—stay with the line of the Blue Ridge escarpment all the way to Blowing Rock, North Carolina, or leave the ridgeline at Fisher's Peak and loop northwest about twenty miles to get across the New River and into the Iron Mountain range in the recently created Unaka National Forest. At Cole's urging and with further encouragement from Clint (C.S.) Jackson, the forest guard for the eastern end of the Unaka National Forest, Avery chose the latter route for the trail. And so, southbound hikers left the Crags and hiked on a paved road to Galax, where they walked right down West Center Street. If, like Earl Shaffer in 1948 (who was headed northbound), they were tired and hungry when they arrived in town, they could pull in at the Bluemont Hotel ("Serving good food at reasonable prices") and spend the night sleeping on clean sheets after a hot shower. If the Bluemont was

THE BLUEMONT HOTEL — GALAX, VA.   2845-30-N

The Bluemont Hotel, Galax, Virginia, in the 1930s. *Author's collection.*

full, there was always the Hotel Waugh just down the street, but the Waugh was said to be haunted by the ghost of a nurse who had perished there in 1904, so the Bluemont was probably a safer choice.

The trail came to Galax in 1931, long before Shaffer hiked through on his way north, and when the trail arrived, the town was still very new as Virginia towns go. Before its official chartering, there had been something like a village at the crossroads now known as Galax, and it wasn't even on the most recent USGS map of the area (1895) when Cole and Ozmer were trying to decide where to run their trail. But by 1930, more than 2,500 people lived in Galax, and that made it the largest town the trail passed through or near between Roanoke and Damascus. Unlike so many towns in Virginia that dated back to colonial times, Galax was the result of industrial, not agricultural, development. Around the turn of the century, two local entrepreneurs formed a land company, hired an engineer from Lynchburg to lay out a town, convinced the Norfolk and Western Railroad to build a spur to the location they had selected along Chestnut Creek and then had a land sale. In just twenty-five years, the town had grown from a vision into a small industrial center, where furniture factories owned by the Vaughns and the Bassetts cranked out dining room suites and another factory "silvered" thousands of mirrors each year. There were sawmills to cut up trees removed from the surrounding mountains, both to supply the furniture mills and to ship lumber north to Roanoke and beyond. There was also a big cotton mill just a few miles away in Fries, but in those days, Fries might as well have been Floyd for all the ease with which a worker might have traveled between the two towns. If you made furniture in Galax, you lived in Galax. If you spun cloth in Fries, you lived in Fries.

Those hikers, and there weren't all that many of them in those days, made a big impression on the good people of Galax when they did stroll through town. Galax was a place where unusual things were, well, unusual. People noticed. And when they did notice, they sometimes called the local paper, the *Galax Gazette*, and reported the unusual happenings. Which is how on July 2, 1951, a reporter was sent out to find "a somewhat unusual tourist… who looked something like Daniel Boone must have looked when he came out of the wilderness." Slightly afraid of the man's beard, because in 1951 a man with a beard was an unusual sight, the reporter sent out to interview "the Walking Man" trailed him into the post office and finally worked up his nerve to conduct an interview with the hiker. That bearded man turned out to be a young man named Gene Espy, who had left Mount Oglethorpe in Georgia (the trail's southern terminus in those days) more than a month earlier and was planning to hike all the way to Maine that summer. Espy, the soul of politeness, patiently explained about his gear, how many miles he walked on an average day and how sometimes he slept in trail shelters or in his tent. He also happily described how many rattlesnakes he had already killed during his hike. If you read Espy's account of his 1951 thru hike—the second such hike after Earl Shaffer's three years earlier—he was a man who believed in killing snakes. Hardly a chapter goes by that a few snakes don't die, usually by a blow from Espy's trusty walking stick. I visited Gene in the summer of 2019, and he let me hold that walking stick. I have to admit that I surreptitiously checked it for signs of snake blood.

That day in 1951, it wasn't the snakes, the fact that he was crazy enough to be planning a hike from Georgia to Maine in one summer or that he liked to sleep in a tent that fascinated the reporter. It was the beard. "He hadn't shaved since he started and does not intend to shave until he completes his trip," the reporter wrote. "Asked if he wasn't afraid he would be tripping on his beard before then, he said he didn't think so, but if it happened, he would just tie it in a knot, thus shortening it." I'm sure the reporter would have been interested to see a photo of Espy when he reached Mount Katahdin that fall. The beard was still there and unknotted.

Gene Espy wasn't the only hiker who wandered down Main Street in Galax and got chased down by local reporters. A few months after Espy

Gene Espy at the conclusion of his thru hike of the Appalachian Trail in 1951. *Personal collection of Gene Espy.*

"The Walking Man" Visits Galax On a 2,050-mile Stroll Monday

Galax had a somewhat unusual tourist for a visitor Monday morning when a heavily bearded young man strolled down Main street with a tremendous pack on his back.

Galax Gazette headline from 1951.

passed through town, Chester Dziengielewski showed up in Galax. In his good-natured way, he answered questions about his hike, which was now nearing its end since he'd begun in Maine back in the spring. The *Galax Gazette* reporter expressed admiration for Dziengielewski's grit in the face of the danger posed by "all the vicious species of wildlife, including snakes, lizards, and various other varmints of the wilderness." Reading that story today, at a distance of more than sixty-five years, it's clear that thru hikers were getting the same questions in 1952 that they get today: Why are you doing this? What do you eat? Where do you sleep? Aren't you afraid of bears, snakes or other critters? How long will it take you?

Dick Lamb and Mildred Norman, who passed through in 1952, were dubbed "Mr. and Mrs. Hiker" by the *Gazette*. The couple rarely disclosed the (unmarried) nature of their relationship and, one imagines, did so even more rarely in the rural South. When the *Gazette* reporter caught up with them in downtown Galax, they had been on the trail a little more than a month and were "tanned and happy and determined" to complete their 2,050-mile hike. They patiently explained that they were taking this long walk to help Lamb get over nervous exhaustion, which the reporter diagnosed as a being a consequence of living in a crazy place like Philadelphia, and that, like long-distance hikers throughout the decades, they had thrown away a fair amount of the gear they had started with, useless things like an alarm clock. They had no tent, preferring instead to sleep on beds made from forest duff, and subsisted mostly on fresh vegetables they bought along their route, as well as oats, peas and beans. Clearly, the reporter was concerned and impressed by the lack of diversity in their diet. And because they were a bit of a novelty, and certainly because they were white, Lamb and Norman reported encountering lots of fine southern hospitality along the trail. I wonder what that reporter would have thought had he learned that Norman changed her name to Peace Pilgrim after completing her thru hike or that she went on to walk more than 25,000 miles with the goal of teaching mankind the ways of peace and nuclear disarmament.

Other than furniture, the biggest thing about Galax—to outsiders, that is—was, and still is, the Old Fiddler's Convention. In the spring of 1935, members of the local Loyal Order of Moose and the Galax High School PTA needed a way to raise some money—and maybe have some fun while they did that. They hit on the idea of holding a fiddlers' convention that would, they hoped, help with "keeping alive the memories and

Old Fiddlers' Convention

Friday, April 12th

7:30 P. M.

High School Auditorium

Galax, Virginia

Tickets for sale by any member of Moose Lodge or by Mrs. Floyd Williams, President of P.-T.A.

GET YOUR TICKETS EARLY

Admission 10c & 25c

Advertisement for the Old Fiddler's Convention in Galax, Virginia. *From the* Galax Gazette, *1935.*

sentiments of days gone by and make it possible for people of today to hear and enjoy the tunes of yesterday." Advertisements in the local papers invited musicians from the surrounding counties to come, play their music in the high school auditorium and win some prizes. No one could have imagined what would happen next or in the years ahead. For ten or twenty-five cents, anyone who wanted to hear some music was invited to come to the high school auditorium for the evening; musicians participating could get in for free. Imagine the surprise of the planners of the event when the crowds were overwhelming. According to the local paper, "The auditorium was filled beyond its capacity, extra chairs were taken in and placed in every available space in the aisles and hundreds stood wherever they could find barely enough room to squeeze themselves in and many of these at great sacrifice of comfort." All told, 897 people paid admission, and another 200 were turned away at the door. Almost 100 musicians filled out the crowd. All this in a town with a stated population of just over 2,500 people. The first "Old Fiddlers' Convention," as they called it then and still call it now, was so successful that they had a second one later that summer. The summer date caught on, and now each year several thousand people came to Galax from around the United States and from overseas for what is billed as the oldest and the world's largest fiddlers' convention.

Except for the hotels, though, Galax was a strange and not very attractive interlude on the trail. The trail went right down West Center Street, but before hikers coming from the north got there, they had to walk past the furniture factories that lined Chestnut Creek; if they were coming from the south, those factories were their last memory of Galax before they headed off toward Fisher's Peak. Why route a hiking trail through the middle of a small town at all? The answer is fairly simple. Cole and Ozmer were anxious to get the trail from the edge of the Great Escarpment up to the Iron Mountain range in the recently formed Unaka National Forest (now part of the Jefferson National Forest), and that meant crossing the New River. In that part of Virginia in 1930, there were only two good options for crossing the river. The new Highway 221 bridge southwest of Galax required southbound hikers (and Cole and Ozmer were scouting in a southbound direction) to bend their route away from the Iron Mountains rather than toward them. The other option was Dixon's Ferry, one of several small ferries across the river, just north of Galax and the bustling mill town of Fries. The ferry option had the advantage of being north of town, which meant hikers had a more direct route between the Iron Mountains and Fisher's Peak, and it was more scenic than just tramping across a highway bridge that carried a fair amount of traffic even in 1930. Another reason for routing the trail through town was so that hikers could resupply and visit a post office before they hit the much more isolated stretch of trail along Iron Mountain. And so, hikers trudged past those factories on their way north to Dixon's Ferry, where they crossed the river the same way people had been crossing it for one hundred years.

CROSSING THE RIVER

My great-grandfather built the ferry. He had a blacksmith shop out back.
He used to "put people across." That's what we called it. They would holler
from across the river and someone would go get them. Daddy or sometimes
Momma would go in the boat.
—Sally (Dixon) Rakes describing her family's ferry
that brought hikers across the New River, 2018

In the summer of 1835, Alexander Dixon brought his wife to the east shore of the New River, just a few miles downstream from Bartlett Falls. Dixon had received a land grant of 3,200 acres on both sides of the river and had come there to carve a farm out of the forests that lined both banks. On the east shore, the land rose up sharply, and it was there that he built the family home, which still stands there today, a neat white house with a bright-green roof. His son added a blacksmith shop, and over the course of two generations, the Dixons cleared enough land across the river to have a substantial farm. There was no road from Galax because there was no Galax—that town wasn't founded until after 1900—so getting back and forth across the river in those days was a personal matter. Family members poled themselves from one side to the other in the distinctive long flat-bottomed skiffs that barely rose twelve inches out of the water and were a common sight on the wide and often shallow New River.

For decades, the Dixons made their living farming, fishing, blacksmithing and making and selling a little moonshine. With each passing year, more

Charles and Warren Dixon, circa 1940. *Personal collection of Paula Rakes.*

people came to the New River Valley to farm, dig for iron and establish small towns. Before long, what had been a mostly wild place upriver from Wytheville had become a string of farming and mining communities. Eventually, a road came down the ridge behind the Dixon family farm to the river just upstream of their home, and the other spur of that road appeared on the opposite shore. It was only natural then that the Dixons would start poling neighbors, tradesmen and others across the river for a modest charge. By 1900, things were happening just upstream. A dam was being built at the falls, and a mill was going to follow. Before long, a town named Fries appeared just below the dam, and people started pouring in to work at the Washington Mill making cotton products. Shortly, a rail spur came down the river valley from Pulaski, dead-ending at Fries, and the Dixons could hear the trains going back and forth every day and could see them when the leaves were off the trees.

The increase in population was good business for the Dixon family. Before long, their little flat-bottomed boats were just a sideshow to a much larger ferry that could carry carts, wagons and eventually cars across the river. Around the same time, Galax appeared just over the ridge and a few miles beyond, and soon more and more people, goods, machinery and whatnot needed to get across the river. By 1930, the Dixons were charging twenty cents for a car, but a hiker could get a ride across the river for a nickel. Business at the ferry remained good until 1940, when the biggest rainstorm anyone could remember blew through the Southern Appalachians and dumped so much rain into the New River that the flood was beyond incredible. "Daddy told me that a Pentecostal church washed away and floated right by the house," Sally (Dixon) Rakes told me in a recent interview. The flood of 1940 also washed away the family's ferry business, which was already in trouble due to the construction of a highway bridge across the river upstream from Fries. As a result, the Dixons abandoned the large ferry but kept bringing hikers and other foot travelers across for a nickel right up until the trail moved away in 1952. That same year, the state finally built a highway bridge across the New River at the site of the family ferry and that was that. Today, all that remains of the ferry business are the strong memories of the Dixon family and the name on the bridge: Dixon's Ferry Bridge.

I learned a lot about Dixon's Ferry in the spring of 2019 from Paula and Sally Rakes. Sally's father was the last member of the family to operate the ferry, and her daughter Paula is the family historian and genealogist. On that beautiful spring afternoon, I sat in their kitchen while their two old dachshunds, one of whom could not keep her tongue in her mouth no matter how hard she tried, shuffled around our feet demanding attention. Sally's memories of the old ferry are very strong, even though she was just a girl when the business closed. "The ferry crossed the river close to the first house there on the road. That's where Momma was raised. Where you see the old deck—that was the blacksmith's shop. William Oliver Dixon was my granddaddy." As the 1941 *Guide to the Paths of the Blue Ridge* noted, "Reach east bank of New River where Dixon Branch empties into it, at 5.2 m. and turn right downstream. At 5.4 m. road to left leads ten yards to river bank at Dixons Ferry over New River. Current is swift; river normally 4 or 5 ft. deep here; old building on right of road is where ferry lands."

The New River is easily seventy-five yards wide at Dixon's Ferry Bridge, so it was a real advantage to be hiking southbound on the Appalachian Trail in those days. All you had to do was walk up to the Dixons' back door, knock and then request a ride across the river. If you were a northbounder, though, you reached the west shore of the river and had to holler across to the other shore until someone at the Dixons' house heard you and poled across in the skiff they called *Redbird* to get you. That's what Gene Espy did in 1951. "I had to yell for quite a while before anyone heard me," he told me in the summer of 2019. Gene was ninety-one when I interviewed him, and while his memories of his hike in 1951 were starting to fade, moments like that one still stood out. I did ask Sally Rakes if her parents had ever thought of installing a bell on the far shore to make it easier for hikers to get someone's attention at the Dixon home. She thought about that for a minute, chuckled and said, "That would have been a good idea."

Hollering across the river is also what Dick Lamb and Mildred Norman did in 1952 when they came through that summer. "I remember a married couple once. They were real nice," Sally Rakes told me. "I remember them because they were a couple. That was very unusual." She didn't know, of course, that Lamb and Norman weren't married at all, as they kept that little detail of their hike to themselves. When they met people along the trail (or a reporter in Galax), Lamb would often go first, saying, "Hi. I'm Dick Lamb and this is Mil," and would let folks assume that the two were married—in 1952, why wouldn't they be? They weren't always that polite about it, though, because the day after they crossed over the river in *Redbird*, they refused to give their names to the local newspaper reporter, a somewhat shocking breach of local manners, which is why he dubbed them "Mr. and Mrs. Hiker."

Not many hikers came this way in the earliest days of the trail. In 1937, it must have been quite a surprise when three hikers—two men and a woman—showed up together asking for passage across the river for themselves and their backpacks. And it must have been an even bigger surprise for the Dixon man giving rides that day to find that the men were doctors from all the way up in Philadelphia named George W. Outerbridge and Martin Kilpatrick. With them was Mary Kilpatrick, Martin's wife, who should be more famous than she is, because it was Mary Kilpatrick who was the first woman to hike every step of the Appalachian Trail. Not Mildred Norman and definitely not Emma Gatewood. Each of these women gets her own place in the Appalachian Trail pantheon—Norman was the first to hike the whole trail in one season (as a "flip flopper") when she and Dick Lamb had a ride across the river in *Redbird*, and Emma Gatewood was the first woman to hike it all in one year all by herself. Those two—Norman and Gatewood—were more than a little quirky, to say the least. The year after her hike, Norman changed her name to Peace Pilgrim, discarded her worldly possessions and went on to walk around the world promoting world peace and nuclear disarmament. Gatewood later became justifiably famous for perhaps being possibly the most determined hiker of all time, almost dying in the first week of her first attempt at a thru hike when she got lost in the wilds of Maine and then coming back the next year to hike it all in Keds, with a denim sack for a backpack, famously subsisting on cans of Vienna Sausages as her primary food group.

Mary Kilpatrick was the opposite of quirky. She was an avid hiker and trail worker. She was a leader of the Philadelphia Trail Club, one of the original Appalachian Trail clubs, regularly organizing group hikes and trail work days throughout central Pennsylvania. And as her husband, Martin, and his friend George began section hiking the Appalachian Trail in earnest, she was their driver, resupply staff and general support person. Along the way, she hiked most of the trail herself, and when they finished, the three of them calculated all the miles Mary had hiked and realized that she was almost done herself. So, the men reversed roles and became her support team until she, too, had hiked every step of the trail herself by the end of 1939. You can still find references to Mary Kilpatrick once in a while in histories of the

Appalachian Trail, but you have to look. In all my searching of the various Appalachian Trail archives, I've only ever found one photograph of her. Although it might look odd today, wearing a stylish hat while out on the trail doesn't exactly qualify as quirky, given that some men in the 1930s took long day hikes wearing a vest and a tie. Maybe if she'd been quirkier we'd know her better. Instead, Mary just hiked, led hikes or helped build trail. And she became the first woman to hike the whole AT.

By contrast, Outerbridge, an active member of the venerable Appalachian Mountain Club and a regular correspondent with Myron Avery, ended up getting a shelter named after him in Pennsylvania. After the Second World War, the Kilpatricks moved to Chicago, where they both became chemistry professors at the Illinois Institute of Technology. They're all but forgotten these days, despite the fact that Outerbridge, in his account of their multi-year section hike, credits the two of them with being the ones who always seemed to be able to find a path for the group through parts of the trail that had fallen into disrepair or weren't yet properly blazed. George might not have made it had it not been for his friends.

When the Kilpatricks and Outerbridge showed up at Dixon's Ferry in 1937, they found it just as the original planners of the trail did. Quiet. Outerbridge later described that brief moment in the only written account

The Kilpatricks, George Outerbridge and an unknown hiker on the AT in Pennsylvania, 1931. *Philadelphia Trail Club Archives.*

of taking the ferry by an Appalachian Trail hiker that I've been able to find, and he didn't say much:

> *The man who runs the ferry across the New River near Galax, Virginia, told us he had been there over three years, but had never before taken any trampers across. Although the white blazes are on fence posts right down his lane, he had no idea of their meaning.*

According to Paula Rakes, granddaughter of the last of the Dixon ferrymen, her grandfather, who was that man who ran the ferry, knew perfectly well what those white blazes meant. It's certainly possible, though, that when the three hikers from up north showed up in 1937, they were the first hikers from outside the area who had asked him to be put across.

The most famous of the early hikers to cross over the New River, of course, was Earl Shaffer, still considered the first thru hiker despite Jim McNeilly's efforts, but he never made it to Dixon's Ferry in 1948; when he did his second thru hike in the 1970s, the trail had long since moved west, crossing the river on a bridge up in Pearisburg. Earl was so confused the afternoon in 1948 when he hiked upstream from Byllesby Dam that he erroneously decided that the trail must have crossed the river in the town of Fries, despite what his trail guide told him. In the draft of his book *Walking with Spring*, Shaffer put his confusion down to having to hike in the pouring rain, but as Jim McNeilly will tell you, Shaffer wasn't the world's greatest navigator, and as his hike progressed, he became prone to taking shortcuts along roads if they seemed to offer a quicker and easier route to the next clear stretch of trail.

In Shaffer's defense, the Appalachian Trail was in pretty terrible shape in 1948. Essentially, no trail work had been done since early 1942, when the trail-maintaining clubs began shutting down their operations due to a lack of trail workers. Every able-bodied man or woman was working, off fighting or training to fight the Japanese, Germans or Italians. Rationing meant that getting gasoline was becoming increasingly difficult, so even getting to the trail was almost impossible. Thus, the trail fell into disrepair, and as mountain trails do, the cat briars, the rhododendrons, the blackberries, the poison ivy and any number of other quick-growing plants soon obscured much of the route. As it turned out, 1948 was the first year of a full-on effort by the clubs to get the trail ship-shape again, but for sure it was nowhere close to that when Shaffer walked through Grayson, Carroll, Patrick and Floyd Counties that summer. In fact, it was the opposite of ship-shape. Even by 1951, when

"Growed Over Trail" in Grayson County, Virginia, 1951. *Personal collection of Gene Espy.*

three men managed to thru hike, large sections of the trail were still hard to follow, especially in the South and *especially* between the New River and Damascus, where the only trail work that anybody did was done by an annual visit of trail workers from outside the area, usually led by Myron Avery, or by USFS workers led by Clint Jackson, who lived near Byllesby Dam. But still, on the day Earl Shaffer approached Dixon's Ferry and Fries, that section of the trail there wasn't overgrown because it ran along the railroad tracks, and the white blazes hadn't yet faded away completely. Earl just missed them and, being more than a little bullheaded, ignored what his trail guide said and hiked past the ferry to Fries.

First, he tried knocking on someone's door to ask directions to the "government trail." Try to imagine, for just a minute, that you are sitting at home on a rainy summer evening when you hear someone's boots on your front steps. This being a part of the world where folks visited their friends regularly and few had telephones to call ahead, you likely wondered who was coming to see you and why you hadn't heard their car or truck come up the drive. Instead of someone you knew, there was a tall, strapping young man, tanned dark by the sun, water streaming off his army poncho and a backpack at his feet, who politely asked you for directions to a trail you'd never heard of. "Appalachian Trail?" Hmmm. According to Shaffer, the woman who answered her door that evening pointed up the hill behind her house and told him that the trail he wanted was up there. So up he went, bushwhacking around in the rain and fading light for an hour before giving up and returning to the road that ran along the railroad tracks.

Next, he wandered into a small store, where the owner likewise had no idea where the Appalachian Trail might be—hadn't heard of it himself—but it was likely that the nice lady thought he meant the Appalachian Power lines that were up on that hill behind her house. She also probably thought Earl was crazy. The man in the store managed to convince Earl to accept a ride into Galax because he was driving there anyway and the weather was just getting worse, so Earl agreed to take that ride, a decision that, many decades later, ignited a controversy—the kind of controversy only an Appalachian Trail thru hiker can really embrace. To a "purist" thru hiker, that ride meant that Earl Shaffer was *not* the first thru hiker after all. He skipped a significant section of trail that evening and thus hadn't hiked the whole thing, thereby making Gene Espy the real first thru hiker in 1951. I asked Gene about this in 2019, and he just smiled and said, "Earl Shaffer was a great man and I'm just glad to be counted in his company." Gene's that way, crediting everything good in his life to God, clean living and a wonderful family. First? Second? That's not why Gene hiked—he hadn't even heard of Earl Shaffer when he started hiking—and it's not why he stayed connected to the Appalachian Trail community all these decades. He hiked for the love of adventure and to see the glory of God's creation made manifest in the mountains of Appalachia. Plain and simple. In fact, Gene learned of Earl and his hike from none other than John Barnard when he stopped at Barnard's house just before venturing over the Pinnacles. In March 2002, Earl Shaffer was in the hospital dying of cancer, and Gene wrote him a sweet letter in which he explained that it was during his stay at the Barnard home that John Barnard told Gene about Earl and showed him some newspaper clippings of Earl's hike. That's where Gene learned that if he made it to Katahdin, he would be the second thru hiker. Later on in his hike north, Gene relished finding little notes that Earl had left in shelters along the way, especially the ones with Bible verses.

Unlike Earl, Gene did take Dixon's Ferry across the New River, and Sally Rakes remembers him, even though she was just a girl that summer. "One year a man came through and he spent a little time chatting with my grandparents. At Christmas time he sent a card with a picture of himself at Mount Katahdin with his walking stick and a beard. He had his beard already when he came to our house. I was a little nervous about that beard." Gene also remembered the Dixons when I spoke with him. "They were very nice people. The river was very wide and I was glad to have a ride across it," he told me.

In the summer of 2019, as they do every summer, the whole extended Dixon family—and there are a lot of them to be sure—gather on the banks of the river on the last little patch of land that a family member still owns. It was a picture-perfect day for a family reunion and a cookout—sunny, hot, the river running as clear as it ever does. Picnic tables were scattered under the shade of the large oaks and cottonwoods that grow right at the point where the land rises up toward the road—Dixon's Ferry Lane. There were some big white picnic pavilions, and families had put up pop-up picnic tents, spread out folding chairs in circles around coolers and in the little house by the road, the kind of place you keep to stay in when you go fishing. There were dozens of dishes of food—salads, hamburgers, hot dogs, fried chicken, biscuits, beans and more than enough dessert for the dozen or so teenagers wandering around in small groups or hanging close to their parents. A copy of Paula Rakes's family history was out on a table for everyone to peruse, and a big "Trump 2020" banner hung from the porch. Paula kept introducing me as the professor who's writing a book about the Appalachian Trail and the ferry. And so, I ate, and I talked and then talked some more. One of Paula's cousins showed me a picture of the biggest flathead catfish I ever hope to see. He caught it just upstream the week before, and it must have weighed sixty pounds. But the most interesting conversation I had was about George Miller, probably the last thru hiker to take the ferry across the New River, back in the summer of 1952, the same year Lamb and Norman came through. Paula's uncle Griggs Dixon drove his car right up into the party because he wasn't in the kind of shape where he could park up on the road and walk down. When he found out that I was writing a book about the old Appalachian Trail route, he waved me over and launched into a story about Miller, whom he remembered meeting all those years ago. "I can't believe he made it all the way to Maine," Uncle Griggs said. "He seemed too old to make it Galax when Daddy put him across. All the way to Maine? Now that's something."

Uncle Griggs wasn't wrong about Miller's age because he was indeed old. What Griggs didn't know was that Miller was a very experienced hiker and a very determined man. Although the trail had already formally moved west in 1953 when Miller, then aged seventy-two, set out on his hike, for unknown reasons he took the old route through Southwestern Virginia. In addition to

George Miller in 1953. *Potomac Appalachian Trail Club Archives.*

meeting members of the Dixon family, Miller stayed at the Barnard home in Meadows of Dan, later writing to John Barnard to inform him that he had made it all the way to Maine and to thank Barnard for his hospitality. As the last thru hiker to take the old route, he was the last one to cross the Pinnacles of Dan, the last one to stop at the shelter on Rocky Knob and the last one to hike up and over Poor Mountain before descending to Mason Cove and then climbing up onto Catawba Mountain to see the sights from McAfee Knob. And Miller was a bit of an innovator when it came to trail gear. Instead of purchasing a backpack, he made his own rig, pictured here, composed of four separate compartments spread from front to back. As he explained in an interview following his hike, that strange-looking rig distributed the weight of the pack evenly across his body and made it easier to stand up straight while he walked. Miller needed lots of room for his gear because he carried more clothes than any thru hiker who has made it as far north as Virginia ever has: five shirts, three pairs of pants, a sweater and an extra pair of boots to change into when his primary pair became wet. And unlike Gene Espy or Earl Shaffer, who spent much of their hike marveling at the beauty of nature, Miller's notebooks were filled with counts of the numbers of mice he saw in shelters, how fast he walked on a particular day and whether or not it rained. To my knowledge, the "Miller Pack" never caught on—at least I've never seen any reference to anyone copying his design—but who can say it wasn't a great idea?

Dixon's Ferry Bridget in 2019. *Author's collection.*

On my five-hour drive home that July afternoon, I reflected on the nature of memory in a place like Dixon's Ferry. The Appalachian Trail was long, long gone, but people there still remembered it, the same way they do just about everything. They didn't know a lot of details, but what they did know they knew very well. But more importantly, the Appalachian Trail is woven into the larger story of the Dixon family. For them, knowing that the Appalachian Trail crossed the river on *their* family's ferry made them inextricably part of the history of the trail and made the trail an inextricable part of the Dixon family story. Dixons have lived along the river there for almost two hundred years now, and until memories fade completely, that ferry will be an essential part of understanding who they are, where they came from and where they are going. They own only one tiny little piece of land now, a far cry from the 3,200 acres that Alexander Dixon acquired so long ago. But they are still Dixons, and that land is, and to them always will be, Dixon land.

You don't need to shout at the top of your lungs to get poled across the river anymore, and you can't see any evidence of the old ferry today. But you can find a geocache at the spot on the western shore where the ferry used to tie up. That cache was placed there not long ago by Paula Rakes, and her online description of the cache reads:

> *The old Dixon Ferry that was owned and operated by Great Grandpa William Oliver Dixon. In addition to the ferry, Grandpa owned and operated a Blacksmith shop which was located across the river at what is now seen as a wooden deck in the edge of the trees. The ferry crossed the river from the Blacksmith shop/deck to the current pastureland where the traveler would pick up the road on to the town of Fries or other locations. This road can now be seen as the drive passing through the edge of the yard, continuing across the New River Trail and becoming the main private entry drive to the highway.*

The ghosts of the Dixon family and the ghosts of the Appalachian Trail still dance together on that river shore. Because the Dixons have a very long memory and are proud to pass those memories on from one generation to the next, they, at least, will remember the Lost Appalachian Trail, even if no one else does.

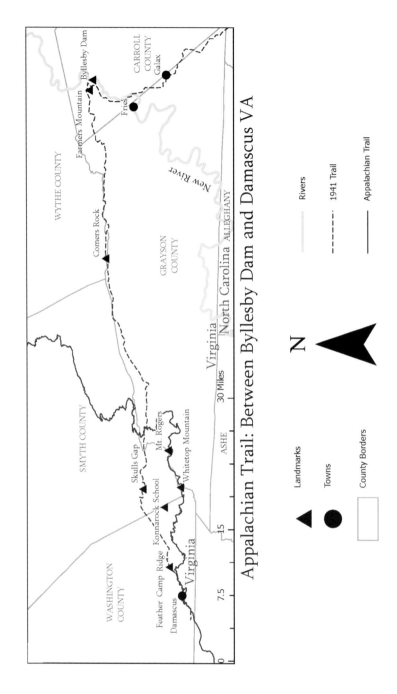

MAP 8 Appalachian Trail between Byllesby Dam and Damascus. *Map created by Timothy Sproule.*

INTO THE WILDS

To put it as simply as possible, a path is a way of making sense of the world.
—Robert Moor, On Trails, *2016*

Sometimes I think the whole New River Valley is cursed, damned by the prospect of prosperity that never quite happens.

If you know anything about the history of Appalachia, it's not news that the great promises of prosperity always turn out to be phantoms, tricksy ghosts that take on solid form just long enough for people to put down roots, maybe believing that *this time* it's going to be like this forever. Build a house, put in a garden, have babies you send to school nearby, get connected to the place, to the river, to the mists that roll down off the mountains into the river valley, to the way the sun lights up the sky and turns the air all around you yellow and orange on summer evenings. And then, whoever has the money, golfs with the regulators in Richmond or Washington or knows the bankers in Chicago, New York or Atlanta decides that they just aren't making enough money here or there and that it's time to take their money somewhere else. The mill closes, the mine is blocked up and the rails that used to bring the trains to town get sold for scrap; then the stores close, the kids have to go to the unified school somewhere an hour or more away and your neighbors and friends have to drive farther and farther to find work. Before long, houses start needing a new coat of paint that they won't get, yards don't get mowed the way they should, families start to fracture and the kids move away once they finish high school.

The Virginia stretch of the New River Valley isn't coal country. It was metals that brought in the prospectors and then the mining companies—nickel, lead, copper, zinc and manganese but most of all iron. More than anything else, it was the iron deposits that brought the out-of-town money into the valley, but most of those mines were small operations, never producing enough to keep the money people interested for long, so towns built to house miners, places like Ivanhoe and Allisonia, flourished for a while and then started to die slowly. All you have to do is drive through those places and see the size of some of the homes to know that once upon a time someone was making real money there. But not anymore.

What didn't go away was the power of the river, power to spin the turbines that created the electricity needed to turn spindles, lift ore out of mines and keep the lights on in the towns up and down the valley. Appalachian Power built or bought the five dams on the river in Virginia, and three of them—Fries, Byllesby and Buck—were visible from the summit of Farmer Mountain if you were hiking the Lost Appalachian Trail. The trail is long gone, of course, but the dams are still there, the river is still spinning their turbines, still pumping power into the grid. That power mostly goes other places now, humming along the high-tension lines to Blacksburg, Roanoke, Radford and beyond into places unknown to the river.

Byllesby Dam from Farmer Mountain in 1951. *Personal collection of Gene Espy.*

Today, this stretch of the New River Valley belongs to paddlers, fishermen, hikers on the New River Trail and people with vacation places along the river, but in 1930, when the Appalachian Trail arrived, from Pulaski to Fries the river valley hummed with industry. Ivanhoe, just north of Byllesby Dam, was a thriving mining town, and the Washington Mill just upstream in Fries employed hundreds of men and women. Norfolk Southern trains came up and down the river, picking up finished linens in Fries or ore from the mines in Carroll, Wythe and Montgomery Counties. But the signs of decline were already there for everyone to see. The mining and smelting operation in Allisonia had gone under two decades earlier, and what was once a thriving small town was fading fast. The operators of the mines at Ivanhoe started scaling back their operations, and the blast furnace had already closed. These days, some people like to say that Ivanhoe's decline was the result of the town being cursed by Methodist circuit rider Robert Sheffey at the end of the previous century. The real reason was that big mines in places like Montana and Wyoming were just producing too much ore at much lower costs, and little operations like the ones in Allisonia and Ivanhoe couldn't complete. It wouldn't be long before Virginia's metals industry mostly became a memory of an earlier industrial revolution, leaving behind rusty hulks of old machinery and toxic tailings on the edge of town.

Hikers on the Appalachian Trail are famous for not noticing much of what goes on in towns they pass through on their way to the trail. To be sure, they stop in those towns to buy supplies and sometimes to spend the night in a rented room, so they see at least something of life there. Anyone planning to hike the trail between Dixon's Ferry and Damascus would likely own a copy of the ATC's *Guide to the Paths in the Blue Ridge*, and the 1934 edition advises that there were a few ways to reach this section of the trail (other than walking): by car from Ivanhoe or Fries or by train, getting off at Byllesby Junction. Anyone planning to purchase last-minute provisions for their hike, or who was passing through on their way north or south, might have been able to purchase a few things in Byllesby, but there wasn't much of a town there, so their options would have been pretty limited. That meant stores in Ivanhoe, Galax or Fries would have been the places to do any of that shopping. Regardless of where they did their shopping, the ATC advised anyone hiking the sixty-six miles between Damascus and Dixon's Ferry to load up on provisions at either end before hitting the trail because the only options for procuring other supplies in this stretch of trail would have been local farmers who might sell some produce to a hiker on "the

Ivanhoe Blast Furnace, circa 1910. *Virginia Tech University Digital Collections.*

government trail." If any of the hikers did stop in Ivanhoe, did they notice that life was headed south there? Probably not. Instead, they would have been much more focused on getting their purchasing done and getting on the trail, just as hikers mostly are today.

Getting to Byllesby Dam from Dixon's Ferry was the easy part because the trail followed alongside the railroad line until it reached Byllesby Junction. At the junction, the trail crossed over the tracks, passed between two cottages and began a steep ascent to the summit of Farmer Mountain (3,040 feet), climbing 1,000 feet in just a little over a mile. From the summit of Farmer Mountain, hikers could see all the way down to Fries and a good bit of the way north up the river valley. On a clear day, Mount Rogers, Virginia's highest peak, was visible to the southwest. Due west, the long spine of Iron Mountain, which extends all the way from the New River to the Doe River just north of Johnson City, Tennessee, beckoned the southbounders. If they were headed north, off to the southeast, they could just make out Fisher's Peak down across the North Carolina border and maybe Buffalo Mountain in Floyd County if the air was really clear. Those kinds of 360-degree views are a rare thing along the Appalachian Trail, and when they do exist, they are rarely so filled with possibility. Even on the gray rainy day when Earl Shaffer crossed the summit, he could see all the way down to the highway bridge south of Galax and felt encouraged. If only he'd known how lost he would get before he made it to that bridge.

Once they'd taken in the views, hikers headed to Damascus had to go back down the mountain, where the trail spent the next six miles or so winding along local roads ranging from paved to almost impassable dirt tracks until it reached the edge of the Unaka National Forest. There on Brush Creek stood the home of Clint Jackson, the "forest guard" of that section of the national forest. Forest guards were seasonal staff of the forest service who an early report of the service describes as "an energetic, enthusiastic lot of men who are willing at all times to perform their duties under the most severe and trying conditions." Jackson, referred to in the old trail guides as "C.S.," was one of Myron Avery's most trusted helpers along the trail in Southwestern Virginia. Whenever he could, Avery much preferred to work with federal government staff like Jackson rather than local volunteers, largely because Avery, a federal worker himself, considered them to be much more dependable when it came to things like locating trail routes, marking the trail and keeping it open. They were also, in his view, much more likely to provide him with the accurate trail data, and that was one of the things he cared most passionately about. Jackson also had serious trail building skills and, from time to time, access to forest service personnel who could help keep the trail open and well marked. Another thing that Avery clearly appreciated about Jackson was that he was more than happy to do what Avery wanted. The archives contain many letters back and forth between the two men, most of them Avery asking Jackson to do this or that on the trail and Jackson writing back that he was more than happy to do what Avery needed or that he already had done what Avery asked. Unlike Shirley Cole, whom Avery found increasingly frustrating to deal with, Jackson, like John Barnard in Patrick County, was a steady, dependable presence, whom Avery could count on to just get things done. And just as importantly for a constant correspondent like Avery, Jackson stayed in touch, responding to Avery's sometimes insistent letters quickly and thoroughly, providing the kind of details about trail distances and conditions that Avery lived for. Jackson also helped hikers with directions and sometimes let them stay in his home, and he was still there when Earl Shaffer passed by in 1948, although by then he had retired from the forest service. The two chatted briefly about farming techniques before Shaffer moved on toward the New River. One wonders what Jackson thought about the idea that Earl was planning to hike all the way to Maine.

From Jackson's house, the trail largely left roads behind, except for the occasional crossing, until it reached Damascus, and it was this stretch that Avery referred to in 1936 as "a no-man's land." Here, at last, the Lost Appalachian Trail entered a region that felt much more like the trail hikers know today: a ridgeline walk, dipping down only to cross a stream or a road and then back up onto the ridge again. Of course, the early incarnations of the Appalachian Trail were not nearly as wild as the trail hikers walk today, as so many of those ridgelines were open pastures for cows, horses and hogs or hayfields for the farms below. This part of Virginia was an important source of wood for the furniture factories in Galax, Bassett and Martinsburg, as well as those in Grand Rapids, Michigan, and elsewhere, and so hikers would have passed through many areas that had been logged off. But there were also large stands of ancient oaks and spruce and dense growths of rhododendron, some with trunks as thick as a man's waist.

Even though much of this stretch of the trail was on national forest lands, because it was much more remote and still in heavy agricultural use between 1930 and 1952, the stretch of trail between Byllesby Dam and Damascus was also the most difficult for those responsible for the Appalachian Trail in Southwest Virginia to take care of. There were few roads that gave access to the trail route, and the ones that existed were often in terrible shape. Farmers in this part of Virginia still piled their hay into tall cones, and hikers often had to cross rickety wooden fences or find a gate. Rather than following white blazes on trees, hikers often looked for cairns or metal Appalachian Trail signs on fence posts. A typical example of directions given to hikers in the trail guides for this section is, "Cross rail fence and go short distance through scrub growth into faint trail through an open field overlooking Francis Mill Creek....Pass rock pile and follow left edge of wire fence with field on left." As Earl Shaffer wrote of the stretch of trail east of Skulls Gap, "Pasture lands continued all day, with marking poor, and camp was pitched in a clump of pines...an early start brought more pastures...many rail fences crisscrossed the grasslands during the afternoon."

Despite, or perhaps because of, the bucolic and largely agricultural nature of the landscape along Iron Mountain in the 1930s and 1940s, hikers often had spectacular views from a promontory or summit. To the north, they could gaze out over the lower Shenandoah Valley and the Holston River watershed, and to the south there was no avoiding the views of Mount Rogers, the highest peak in Virginia at 5,729 feet, and its next-door neighbor, Whitetop (5,518 feet). Although the forest has reclaimed

The view from Comer's Rock in 2009. *From the* Appalachian Voice.

the ridgeline today, one can still have wonderful views of these two great mountains and get a good sense for the landscape the trail traverses these days through the Mount Rogers National Recreation Area. In 1932 or 1952, summiting Mount Rogers or Whitetop meant driving or taking the narrow-gauge rail line up to Whitetop station rather than following white blazes through the forest and past the wild ponies that are such an attraction to hikers now. When ATC- or PATC-sponsored work crews would come down to the area for work weekends, the lodge on Whitetop was where they stayed. The old lodge is long gone, of course, like so much of the human history of the region, but back in the day it was famous for its fried chicken and fruit pies.

Hikers can walk the old route of the trail today by finding the eastern terminus of the Iron Mountain Trail just south of Brush Creek (Trail 301 on the maps of the Mount Rogers National Recreation Area and the Jefferson National Forest) and hike west toward Dry Run Gap and Highway 21. The Iron Mountain Trail mostly (but not always) follows the old Appalachian Trail route. If you do hike along the old trail today, you'll pass through a region where the understory is still filling in, where lush fields of large ferns dominate beneath the rapidly growing timber. You'll pass by crumbling lengths of stone fence glimpsed back in the forest, and if you look carefully, from time to time will see a few fence posts with rusted bits of barbed wire, a reminder that not too long ago much of this land was still the domain of pigs, cattle and sheep.

Before 1952, hikers walking south left Brush Creek and ascended to the summit of Jones Knob (3,820 feet), dropping down briefly into a gap to cross a road that used to but no longer bisects the mountain. From there they climbed again, this time to the summit of Perkins Knob (3,852 feet) and then back down hill to U.S. Highway 21, one of the two major roads that crossed the trail's route along Iron Mountain and so one of the only easy access points for trail workers coming down from Washington, Roanoke and Lynchburg to work with the crews from the forest service and later the CCC, who built this section of trail. The lack of any sort of local trail club to build and then watch over the trail in Grayson and Washington Counties meant that "flying squads" from the north or forest service staff did much of that work. A 1936 description from the Potomac Appalachian Trail Club *Bulletin* of what it was like to be on one of those flying squads—down from Washington, D.C., Roanoke and Lynchburg for a weekend of trail work—reads:

> *Heading westward along the ridge we were glad to stretch our legs on the sharply ascending path. To the southwest rose a magnificent shoulder of Mt. Rogers, culminating in a crest dark with conifers. We skirted upland meadows for several miles, and then entered a splendid stand of mature hardwood timber toward the summit of Flat Top, where ferns grew waist-high between the huge trunks. In spite of a stop to admire a baby partridge which one of us captured temporarily, we covered the nine miles to Skulls Gap at a brisk gait, reaching the bus in time to see a superb sunset from the side of Whitetop while on our way to spend the night at the lodge near the summit....Trail measuring and marking along three miles of the AT north of [Houndshell Gap] occupied us till the early evening. Some of us thought the sweeping views from the high grassy ridges along this section the best we had seen on the trip.*

When Myron Avery described this region of Virginia as "terra incognita" back in 1930, more than anything else, he meant these stretches of Iron Mountain. The region wasn't really unknown, of course, just unknown to Myron Avery up in Washington, D.C. White settlers had lived here for almost two hundred years, and for many centuries before that the Cherokee had been using these forests for their own purposes. Many of the ridgetops

Feathercamp Mountain fire tower in 1953. *U.S. Forest Service Archives.*

were balds suitable for grazing livestock. During the Civil War, they turned out to be good places to hide one's horses from Union army troops who arrived in the region toward the end of the war—or, if one opposed the war, hiding from Confederate army press gangs, as some men did around Comer's Rock. Until just before the arrival of the trail, massive chestnut trees dominated many of the mountainsides, providing pig farmers with ideal ranges for their hogs. The lumber industry in nearby Damascus and Whitetop just south of Mount Rogers brought in hundreds of workers to cut, peel and process the chestnut and oak trees that grew with abandon along the steep ridges. These days, those huge trees are almost all gone, largely replaced by Christmas tree farms that dot the steep slopes. There is something a little disconcerting about all those long, well-ordered rows of small firs carpeting slopes that once were thick with wild hardwoods. Somehow it's all just too orderly and neat.

The original planners of the Appalachian Trail in this area—Avery, Jackson and U.S. Forest Service supervisor C.L. Graham—chose a route that provided excellent scenic views, challenging climbs and access to the forest service's chain of fire towers on Jones Knob, Comers Rock (4,035 feet) and Feathercamp Mountain. Each of these towers had an access road for the tower keeper, which made access by trail workers, and later hikers, much easier and more dependable. Being a tower keeper in such a remote location was a somewhat lonely profession, and certainly the appearance of a lone hiker, or a few in the case of the Kilpatricks and George Outerbridge in 1937, must have livened up the days of the tower keepers. Several hikers before 1953 reported receiving warm welcomes from the tower keepers, although sometimes they were greeted by a "No Visitors" sign at the base of the tower and so just kept walking.

Like so much of this part of Virginia, the hollows and water gaps of the Iron Mountain range are filled with stories. For example, if you drive west from Elk Creek, you'll see a VDOT historical marker about a little girl, Caty Sage, who at age five was kidnapped by a local settler who then sold her to a local Cherokee band in 1792. Caty's Cherokee captors then gave her in trade to a Wyandot tribe from Ohio who named the little girl Yourowquanins. Over the decades, Yourowquanins rose to a position of prominence among the Wyandots, and when U.S. government troops drove them out of Ohio, she helped lead the trek to Kansas, where they settled for good. In one of the more remarkable coincidences of American history, one of Caty's brothers had come to Kansas from Virginia, and at a trading post on the Kansas border, he learned that a white woman with a facial scar similar to his stolen sister's lived nearby. Although she spoke no English, through a translator they established that Yourowquanins was his long-lost sister Caty, abducted fifty-six years earlier. A children's book, a few Facebook posts and that VDOT marker are all that remain of the story of Caty Sage, but if you chat with people in the area, one of the first things they ask is, "You know the story of Caty Sage, don't you?" And then they tell you the story as though it happened in 1992, not 1792.

The story of Caty Sage is perhaps the most exciting tale I ran across west of the New River, but there are so many small stories in these mountains that I would love to get to the bottom of and never will. One that sticks with me concerns a certain man, not a real man, sitting in a small shelter by a farm gate in Cripple Creek. I was driving from Elk Creek to Grant on a beautiful October day in 2018, tracking the route of the old trail from down below the ridgeline, and saw two picturesque old barns on the hillside beyond a gate. They were so beautiful there on the side of the hill that I had to turn around and pull off so I could take a picture. Next to the gate was the kind of shelter that many rural homes have for schoolchildren to sit in while waiting for the school bus on a foul weather morning. I was so fixated on those barns that I paid no attention to the shelter as I walked up to the gate. But when I turned around, I almost jumped out of my hiking boots, as there was a man inside, sitting there, staring at me through a sheet of plexiglass. After a few deep breaths, I realized that he was a mannequin, resplendent in a big Stetson hat, old jeans, a concho belt and scuffed cowboy boots. That shed he was in was actually an old outhouse that had been repurposed as a gatehouse to play jokes on nosy photographers like me, or just to keep life a little more lighthearted for the family who lived on the farm. Southwestern Virginia is like that. Just when you think you know the place, it surprises you.

Other than the fire towers, the road crossings and a few small churches like the Comer's Creek Baptist Church that one could see from up on the ridge, there weren't many landmarks for hikers between Skulls Gap and Damascus, with the important exception of the old Konnarock Training School. Founded in 1924, the Konnarock School was there to provide a Christian education and employable skills to poor children in the nearby mountain communities. Most of the mountain mission schools of that era came and went with regularity because they depended on the support of a local congregation and the volunteer or very low-paid labor of a teacher or two willing to minister to the needs of children, especially girls, in the isolated communities of Appalachia.

Comer's Creek Baptist Church in 2018. *Author's collection.*

By contrast, the Konnarock Training School had the advantage of substantial financial support from the local lumber company and the Women's Missionary Society of the United Lutheran Church, so it survived for three decades, closing just a few years after the Appalachian Trail moved away. At its most active, more than thirty girls lived at the school, and their parents paid either in cash or in barter for their children's education. But like the many other small schools that dotted the route of the old trail in Southwestern Virginia, the Konnarock School eventually became the victim of the improvement in the local road system and the consolidation of schooling by local counties. Once it was possible, or at least easier, for poor children to reach consolidated schools on improving roads, one- and two-room schools began closing all over the region and the need for the mountain mission schools declined. The Konnarock School held on longer than most, but the decline of the local lumber industry after World War II meant that regional boomtowns like Konnarock were doomed. The old school still stands because the forest service renovated it in the 1970s following the creation of the Mount Rogers National Recreation Area, and it became a place where trail workers would sleep while working on trails in the Recreation Area, including, of course, the current route of the Appalachian Trail. The Konnarock Crew, one of the ATC's floating service crews, is named for the old school, and today the school site is home to the Blue Ridge Discovery Center, an outdoor educational center for children, which I think would have made the school's founders very happy.

After southbound hikers passed the Feathercamp Mountain fire tower, it was a quick jaunt down to Damascus, another lumber town that today is best known to hikers as the home of Trail Days, the biggest and increasingly most controversial hiker event along the Appalachian Trail. Walking through Damascus today, one can still see hints of what it looked like when the Appalachian Trail first arrived in the 1930s. Some of the old storefronts on Laurel Avenue still look like they might have been there when the first hikers began coming up from Tennessee or down from Iron Mountain, but the town itself looks nothing like the one those early hikers found when they arrived. For one thing, a hiker today can choose from

Konnarock Training School in 1997. *U.S. Forest Service Archives.*

Damascus Station, Damascus, Virginia, 1948. *Virginia Tech University Digital Collections.*

more than a dozen different hotels, inns, bed-and-breakfasts or rental rooms in an Airbnb and can eat at any one of a dozen diners, restaurants and pizza parlors. In 1932, hikers had only one option recommended to them in the ATC trail guide: "Excellent lodging and meals obtainable in Damascus at the home of Mrs. J.A. Saul." When Gene Espy arrived in 1951, he famously spent the night in the town jail, just like Otis in the old *Andy Griffith Show* (although without any liquor on his breath).

I think it's fair to say that today there is no town along the Appalachian Trail more dependent on hikers than Damascus. When the Appalachian Trail arrived in town around 1930, the population was more than double what it is today, with many good jobs generated by the lumber industry. Today, 20 percent of the population of town (estimated in 2019 at 775) lives in poverty. Without the thousands of sweaty, hungry, tired Appalachian Trail hikers looking for a hot meal, a shower, a cold beer and a real bed to sleep in, Damascus would be a lot like Fries today—a beautiful but faded town along a river where people remember better days. But the hikers do come, and they come in droves and spend plenty of money, especially during Trail Days, an annual event that began more than thirty years ago and has the economic impact of a NASCAR race. The town is quite literally overrun. When I was in Damascus in mid-March 2020, everyone was on edge because the entire country was shutting down due to COVID-19, and folks in Damascus were worried that their big event would be canceled (it was). One local business owner I spoke with told me that times were hard enough and that if Trail Days didn't happen, she wasn't sure she could stay open. I haven't been back to see if she survived, but Trail Days has resumed and resumed with a vengeance.

In the first decades of the trail's history, hikers were a curiosity in Damascus, not a necessity. Originally known as Mock's Mill, the town only became Damascus in 1886, when former Confederate general John Imboden purchased it and renamed the place for the city in Syria. By 1910, Damascus had become one of the main lumber entrepots in the region, and almost all of the trees cut in the vast valley between Mount Rogers and Iron Mountain passed down temporary rail lines into Damascus and from there into the rail net running up and down the Shenandoah Valley. So much timber was cut in the region that by 1912, Grayson and Washington Counties produced more lumber than the entire state of Pennsylvania—and almost all of that lumber passed through Damascus. No wonder hikers were nothing more than an afterthought when they first started showing up.

Over time, though, Damascus became an important jumping-off point or stopping point for hikers passing north and south, and with the advent of Trail Days—which for years was little more than small gathering with a silly parade—the stature of Damascus as a trail town began to grow. The importance of trails for Damascus increased in the late 1980s with the founding of the Virginia Creeper Trail, a rails-to-trails multi-use trail catering to bikers as well as hikers. The town is also the southern terminus of the Iron Mountain Trail—the old route of the AT. A recent economic development study attributed almost two-thirds of the town's revenues to hikers visiting town to access one of these trails. These days, most of the Appalachian Trail hikers who arrive in Damascus come up from the south because northbound hiking somehow became the norm back in the 1960s. Unlike Gene Espy, though, they don't have to sleep in the town jail, nor do they have to look up someone like Mrs. Saul to buy a meal.

Benton MacKaye certainly would have been happy to see how the whole concept of the Trail Town has caught on along the trail he proposed. What we remember today is that MacKaye is the father of America's oldest and most iconic long-distance hiking trail. What we forget is that he was a regional planner, deeply concerned by the plight of small rural communities. His vision for the Appalachian Trail was that it would be the most important piece of a larger project in regional development, a project that would help create or sustain a series of recreational communities throughout the Appalachian chain—communities that would be linked to one another by a walking trail. Damascus is exactly that. Fries or Meadows of Dan or Fancy Gap or Bent Mountain *could* have been one of those connected communities. But Myron Avery and the Appalachian Trail leadership took the trail away, and with it they took the promises of economic development that MacKaye envisioned for communities like them.

TRACES OF THE PAST

The physical traces of the past lie all around, manifest to a greater or lesser degree, ready to be incorporated into what comes next.
—William Turkel, The Archive of Place, *2007*

The original route of the Appalachian Trail in Southwestern Virginia was formally abandoned at the end of the 1952 hiking season, but the seeds of its demise began in the late 1930s. At the 1937 meeting of the Appalachian Trail Conference in Gatlinburg, Tennessee, U.S. Forest Service staffer Edward Ballard proposed a formal agreement between the forest service and the ATC for the ongoing protection and maintenance of the Appalachian Trail in the national forests. Ballard's proposal, which ultimately became the 1938 Appalachian Trailway Agreement, provided for a one-hundred-foot-wide protected strip of land on either side of the trail and for the forest service's help in building and maintaining shelters at reasonable intervals along the trail. Having federal protection for the trail, most of which still crossed private lands or was routed along roads, was highly desirable to the trail community for all the obvious reasons. Any compromises Avery and his allies would have to make with federal officials seemed far outweighed by the prospect of federal protection for the trail. Moreover, at that same Gatlinburg meeting, the ATC committed itself to building a chain of shelters, to be located about eight to ten miles apart, from Maine to Georgia. The prospect of the various trail clubs having to build upward of 250 such structures was daunting to say the least, and obtaining forest service assistance with this task was not just welcome—it was essential.

At the same time that the Trailway Agreement was being worked out, the Jefferson (formerly Unaka) National Forest was growing at a spectacular rate. In 1935, the Jefferson National Forest encompassed some 180,000 acres in Southwestern Virginia, Western North Carolina and Northeastern Tennessee. By 1940, the national forest had ballooned to include more than 550,000 acres. Most significantly for Virginia's Lost Appalachian Trail, some of that growth in the forest was just south and west of Roanoke, which meant that it was possible to move the trail to the west to put it almost entirely on federal land. And that was exactly what Avery, the ATC Board of Managers and the leadership of the Roanoke Appalachian Trail Club decided to do in 1940. Had it not been for what Avery called "the present emergency" (i.e., World War II), work on the trail's relocation would have begun that same year. Instead, as Avery wrote in the ATC's *Trailway News*, relocation would begin once conditions returned to normal and the trail clubs could focus on such things as route finding and trail building. Those "normal" conditions did not return until the early 1950s, when ATC vice-president James Denton reported that with the help of forest service staff and members of the RATC, he had laid out a new route for the trail that turned west from Mason's Cove (rather than south toward Bent Mountain), crossing the New River at Pearisburg and then reconnecting with the old route of the trail on Iron Mountain northeast of Damascus. The board of managers approved his report, and in 1953, hikers were being directed to this new route. The old trail route, with the exception of those last few dozen miles on Iron Mountain, had ceased to exist, at least in the minds of the trail's managers and maintainers.

Myron Avery did not live to see the new route of the trail because he died of a heart attack during the summer of 1952 at the age of fifty-three. Someone once said of Myron Avery that when he died, he left behind two trails: the Appalachian Trail and a trail of bruised egos. One of the reasons Avery rubbed so many people the wrong way was that he was not one to admit error, ever, and the way he handled the old route of the Appalachian Trail in Southwestern Virginia provides ample evidence of his willingness to bend reality to meet the needs of the moment. In 1929, Avery shifted easily from doing his best to forestall Shirley Cole's efforts to route the trail through Floyd and Patrick Counties to making it seem as though it was all his (Avery's) idea. The planned relocation of the trail that began in 1940 makes it even more evident how easily Avery could contradict himself to avoid being wrong.

In the June 1932 edition of *Appalachia*, the journal of the Appalachian Mountain Club, Avery wrote of this section of the trail: "For frequency and expansiveness of panoramic outlooks, this section is unparalleled. In the Dan River Gorge and its Pinnacles the region contains the most outstanding single spectacular feature of the entire Appalachian Trail, with the exception of its northern terminus, Katahdin." He went on to say that given the great scenic beauty of the area, the trail from Roanoke to the New River would follow the eastern rim of the Great Escarpment. Somehow, by 1940, all those advantages had evaporated. "Below Roanoke the narrow crest-line Blue Ridge expands into an enormous plateau. On it there are streams, swamps, patches of woodland, mountaineer's farms and spasmodic cultivation. Only when one comes to the eastern edge of this curving plateau does one realize he is on top of a broad mountain," Avery wrote in the *Trailway News* in 1940. To further explain his reasons why the trail needed to leave this region, Avery explained, "A decade ago the attitude of the people in this region toward strangers was not a particularly friendly one." But in that 1932 article, he invited hikers to the region by saying, "This section is noted for its general hospitality." In other words, in 1932, the trail east of the New River had many wonderful geographic features and the local residents welcomed hikers, but by 1940, those same features were dull and boring and the locals were not particularly friendly. Anyone who has studied the history of Appalachia knows that Avery's willingness to extoll the virtues of the region one day while dismissing those same virtues just a few years later is sadly typical of the many ways the people of Appalachia have been treated over the past one hundred years.

In the end, Avery and the ATC leadership did not decide to move the trail fifty miles west just because of any geographic or cultural factors in Floyd, Patrick or Carroll Counties. The real reasons were more prosaic. As Avery mentions in his 1940 essay on the trail's relocation, the reality was that the Blue Ridge Parkway had all but obliterated the best parts of the trail in this region (with the exception of the Dan River Gorge), and so the trail as it existed in 1940 largely zigzagged back and forth across the parkway. Although this is exactly what happened in Shenandoah National Park at this same time, the difference between the two locations was that in Shenandoah, when the trail left Skyline Drive, it dove back into the forest. In Southwestern Virginia, when the trail left the parkway, it largely followed along roads—roads that were increasingly being improved to accommodate visitors to the parkway. Almost as important, though, was Avery's ongoing frustration over his inability to encourage the formation of a permanent local trail maintaining organization. The RATC was happy to maintain the trail as far south as Adney Gap, John Barnard was a dependable maintainer of the trail from Tuggles Gap to the point where the trail reached the parkway again near Bell Spur Church and Clint Jackson could be counted on to watch over the trail between the New River and Skulls Gap. But when Shirley Cole left the area following his divorce, the nascent trail clubs he had founded fell apart and never managed to reconstitute themselves. That meant Avery was regularly organizing "flying squads" of volunteers from the Washington, D.C. area, Lynchburg, Roanoke and even Kingsport, Tennessee, to help maintain the trail in this region. Given the limitations on transportation in the 1930s and the realities of the Great Depression, that was not a feasible long-term strategy. Thus, when the forest service offered up the possibility of moving the trail onto federal lands in the Jefferson National Forest, Avery jumped at the chance to solve many problems at once.

The arrival of the Second World War meant that all work on the Appalachian Trail had to be scaled back, and after Pearl Harbor, most of the trail maintaining clubs either ceased trail work or curtailed their operations to the barest of minimums. After the war, the trail was largely overgrown and littered with downed trees, rock slides and all the other natural events that drive trail maintainers to distraction. In 1948, Earl Shaffer reported that much of the trail remained overgrown and difficult to follow, and in 1951, Gene Espy, not a man to complain, found a number of sections of the trail "growed over" and difficult to follow. Given these challenges, it is perhaps no surprise that it took until 1952 for the ATC to formally relocate the trail away from its original route to the one it largely follows today.

The Appalachian Trail left its original route in Southwestern Virginia at the end of the 1952 hiking season and quickly passed out of the knowledge of the vast majority of the Appalachian Trail community. Because it was written out of the trail guides, hikers passing north and south in ever-growing numbers had no way to learn that they were missing out on the Pinnacles of Dan, the climb up Farmer Mountain with its 360-degree views or the opportunity to see the second-highest waterfall in Virginia up on Bent Mountain. But the trail left many traces on the landscape of this region, some of which are still easily read today. The Galax chapter of the Daughters of the American Revolution is the "Appalachian Trail" chapter, although the current local DAR leaders aren't sure why. Several roads still bear the name "Appalachian Trail," and if you know where to look, you can find rusty old Appalachian Trail markers on trees, likely put there by Shirley Cole and Myron Avery back in 1931. Those are the tangible things.

The intangible things are just as important. All of us have a place. A place where we feel the most connected, the most comfortable, the place where we know the way things smell, how the wind blows, how people talk and what everyone is eating. Even in this seemingly rootless world, where jet planes shuttle millions through the air every day, where people move with increasing frequency in search of jobs, of water, of security, to get away from war, fire or famine, most humans are still rooted in *their* places, the places they've named, the places they know best. In the South, that place isn't just a place—it's the homeplace. "What's your homeplace?" "This is my homeplace." And homeplaces are endowed with even greater significance than ordinary locations. Every homeplace, wherever it is, has its own stories. Over there, that's where lightning hit the tree.…Right here, that's where we first met.…Up there on the mountain, there's where those folks were lost for three days.…You can see it down there, where the river bends, that's where our neighbor's son found a dead bear. Places become a code, a shorthand for stories that define who we are, who we've been and who we'll be. Physical geography, buildings, soundscapes, smells—they provide the boundaries, the parameters for memory, for understanding, for teaching and, most of all, for belonging.

But just as important as those physical things, if not more so, are the stories—the stories the Dixon family members tell about poling hikers across the river in *Redbird*, Ralph Barnard's tales of hikers and their fear of panthers, the hope that Richard Farmer still holds out for Fries, Dorothy Shifflet's stories of building trail with her father and the pride in Doug Bell's voice when he speaks of how the Appalachian Trail came to his grandfather's front door. In a part of America where the past really matters, the Appalachian Trail lives on, inscribed on the inner landscapes of the people who still remember and are determined not to forget. In this Appalachian heartland, where people's lives are organized around stories of the past and how that past is inextricably woven into their present and their future, memories of the Appalachian Trail and their place in its history remain an important way that they make sense of their world. They wish other people remembered it the way they do, but in the end, all that really matters is that *they* remember the old trail.

BIBLIOGRAPHY

Adkins, Leonard M. *Along Virginia's Appalachian Trail*. Charleston, SC: Arcadia Publishing, 2009.

Anderson, Larry. *Benton MacKaye: Conservationist, Planner, and Creator of the Appalachian Trail*. Baltimore, MD: Johns Hopkins University Press, 2002.

Basso, Keith. *Wisdom Sits in Places: Landscape and Language Among the Western Apache*. Albuquerque, NM, 1996.

Bryson, Bill. *A Walk in the Woods: Rediscovering America on the Appalachian Trail*. New York: Anchor Books, 2006.

Catte, Elizabeth. *What You Are Getting Wrong About Appalachia*. Cleveland, OH: Belt Publishing, 2018.

D'Anieri, Philip. *The Appalachian Trail: A Biography*. New York: Mariner Books, 2021.

Decker, Sarah Jones. *The Appalachian Trail: Backcountry Shelters, Lean-Tos, and Huts*. New York: Rizzoli, 2020.

Eller, Ronald D. *Uneven Ground: Appalachian Since 1945*. Lexington: University of Kentucky Press, 2013.

Espy, Gene. *The Trail of My Life*. Chicago: Indigo Publishing Group, 2008.

Hare, James R. *Hiking the Appalachian Trail*. 2 vols. Emmaus, PA: Rodale Press, 1975.

Harris, Nelson. *A History of Back Creek: Bent Mountain, Poages Mills, Cave Spring and Starkey*. Charleston, SC: The History Press, 2018.

Johnson, Thomas R. *From Dream to Reality: History of the Appalachian Trail*. Harpers Ferry, VA: Appalachian Trail Conservancy, 2021.

Kelly, Mills. "The Class of '51." *Appalachia* (Summer/Fall 2020): 24–33.

King, Brian B., and Bill Bryson. *The Appalachian Trail: Celebrating America's Hiking Trail*. New York: Rizzoli, 2012.

Mittlefehldt, Sarah. *Tangled Roots: The Appalachian Trail and American Environmental Politics*. Seattle: University of Washington Press, 2013.

Montgomery, Ben. *Grandma Gatewood's Walk: The Inspiring Story of the Woman Who Saved the Appalachian Trail*. Chicago: Chicago Review Press Inc., 2014.

Moor, Robert. *On Trails*. New York: Simon & Schuster, 2016.

Ryan, Jeffrey H. *Blazing Ahead: Benton MacKaye, Myron Avery, and the Rivalry that Built the Appalachian Trail*. Boston: Appalachian Mountain Club Books, 2017.

Slavishak, Edward. *Proving Ground: Expertise and Appalachian Landscapes*. Baltimore, MD: Johns Hopkins University Press, 2018.

Turkel, William. *The Archive of Place: Unearthing the Pasts of the Chilcotin Plateau*. Vancouver, CA: UBC Press, 2008.

INDEX

ABOUT THE AUTHOR

Mills Kelly is a professor of history at George Mason University in Fairfax, Virginia, and is a historian of the Appalachian Trail. He began hiking on the trail as a young Boy Scout in 1971, and the trail has been part of his life ever since. Today, he is the maintainer of the Manassas Gap shelter along the trail in Northern Virginia and is the volunteer archivist of the Potomac Appalachian Trail Club. In addition, he is the host of *The Green Tunnel* podcast, a podcast on the history of the Appalachian Trail. The author of several books, he is the executive director of George Mason's award-winning Roy Rosenzweig Center for History and New Media and has won numerous university, state, national and international awards for his teaching. Mills lives in Manassas, Virginia, but also part time in Linden, Virginia, less than a mile from the Appalachian Trail.

Visit us at
www.historypress.com